Heartlines

Heartlines

The Year I Met My Other Mother

Susannah McFarlane & Robin Leuba

VINTAGE BOOKS

Australia

Some of the names of people in this book have been changed to protect their privacy, and the chronology of some events has been altered.

A Vintage book
Published by Penguin Random House Australia Pty Ltd
Level 3, 100 Pacific Highway, North Sydney NSW 2060
www.randomhouse.com.au

 Penguin
Random House
Australia

First published by Vintage in 2016

Addresses for the Penguin Random House group of companies can be found at global.penguinrandomhouse.com/offices.

National Library of Australia
Cataloguing-in-Publication entry

ISBN 978 0 14378 024 3 (paperback)

Adoptees – Australia – Biography
Birthmothers – Australia – Biography
Mothers and daughters – Australia – Biography
Adoptees – Australia – Family relationships
Interpersonal relations – Australia

Other Creators/Contributors: Leuba, Robin, author

362.734092

Front cover photo courtesy Susannah McFarlane; heart © Shutterstock
Back cover photo: Rebecca Bana Photography
Cover design by Nada Backovic
Typeset by Midland Typesetters, Australia
Printed in Australia by Griffin Press, an accredited ISO AS/NZS 14001:2004
Environmental Management System printer

Penguin Random House Australia uses papers that are natural, renewable and recyclable products and made from wood grown in sustainable forests. The logging and manufacturing processes are expected to conform to the environmental regulations of the country of origin.

For my Mum, Gerie

Contents

Preface

Susannah

I didn't really mean to write this book. I write children's books, in particular adventure stories about a little girl being brave; I never thought I'd write anything like a memoir, let alone one with my birth mother.

My life would not make for a great read – most of it has been much too happy, filled with wonderful family and friends, comfort and opportunity, being loved and loving. Then, at nearly fifty, something happened that would bring me right back to where I began and I, too, became a little girl who had to be brave. It started almost accidentally, triggering an emotional journey that would take me to the very heart of my identity, of me.

This is that story; it's also an adventure story, not of my life, but of one year.

The year I met my other mother.

I

START AND FINISH

The mother

Robin

I could hear my voice, strangely detached from me, roaring in the drugged darkness. The bellow of an animal caught up in some sort of universal, impersonal cataclysm of nature. Then, blackout. End of scene. Hours later, I awoke, as if from a dream.

And so it was here, in St Andrew's Hospital, Melbourne, on 14 July 1965, that I gave birth to my first child. For me, there was no visible product to testify to the objective reality of the birthing experience. No sign of a baby. I was still just Robin, pretty much as before: one, indivisible, alone. Yes, there were bodily changes and medical procedures, but they were all still me-centred, self-contained, self-preoccupied. Awake from a dream, but unawakened. Sleeping Beauty slumbering in an emotional time capsule.

Well, here was the problem, or part of it at least. This dreamlike state of disengagement from reality didn't begin with the surreal, drugged-out labour.

I didn't even know I was pregnant till I was five months along, despite suffering classic symptoms of cessation of periods and nausea. To try to explain how such naivety was even possible in a 22-year-old woman, I need to describe the social and cultural milieu of Perth, Western Australia – which is where I and my sisters, Pam and Susan, grew up and where I was attending university at the time I became pregnant.

Perth was a provincial society, isolated from the more cosmopolitan 'eastern states' as we called them. The rules of middle-class respectability were conventional and rigid, and while 'nice girls' could flirt and tease, they certainly did not 'cross the line' before they were married. 'Sexual intercourse' and 'unwed mothers' were terms spoken of in a whisper and shrouded in an aura of dark mystery.

So, back to Robin Leuba, in 1964: twenty-two, a university student, falling in love with Tim, also studying Arts at uni. Two years younger than me, Tim charmed with his flair and wit and we frolicked together on the beaches and in the beer gardens of Perth and in the flat I had recently moved into with two girlfriends, where I indeed confirmed my parents' fears by 'getting into trouble'.

I do not place all the blame for my incredible naivety on the social mores of the time – such extreme dumbness was surely my own work – but I did go to our family doctor about my nausea and loss of periods, and he did not enlighten me. After examining me, he asked me if I could be pregnant, but I looked him in the eye and with total conviction said 'no'. In my mind I could not be pregnant because I had not met the basic requirement – surely what Tim and I had done on the floor of my flat didn't qualify as that forbidden, earth-shattering event, sexual intercourse? (Granted, in the particular circumstances, conception was a long shot, but clearly not impossible.) The doctor knew my parents and was disinclined to rock the boat of respectable society. I suppose he thought he was being tactful and that surely I would get the message from his indirect hints, but he obviously was not aware of the solidity of my delusion. He proceeded to talk about boyfriends and choosing one of them to marry. I honestly had no idea what he was on about. He prescribed some anti-nausea pills and sent me on my way. When I rang him about three weeks later to say the pills had worked but I still didn't have my period, he still kept silent. So, I did nothing and, for me, the first half of my pregnancy was unrealised, and therefore unreal. It was not till I was about five months' pregnant and still didn't have a period that the fear of the 'impossible' struck me and I knew I had to check it out further.

I told Tim my fears and he drove me to see another doctor in the outer suburbs, far removed from any family connections and therefore less likely to be so socially squeamish. Indeed, he was brutally honest: he confirmed that I was at least five months' pregnant, and by his harsh and disdainful manner, he made it clear that he held me in moral contempt.

In shock, Tim and I drove to a hotel to have a drink: we needed time to take in our situation before we had to return home. We sat down in the lounge and, in a characteristic gesture of bravado, Tim ordered champagne. It was perhaps a sentimental gesture, not connected to any practical plan for the future but, if only for that moment, there wasn't a problem, there was something to celebrate. We had made a baby together and there was something special about that. For that hour in the ladies' lounge of that suburban Perth hotel, we were in our own little bubble of wonder.

The bubble, of course, had to burst. The next morning I broke the news to my mother.

Mum was sitting up in bed with her morning cup of tea when I told her. I can still see the look of crushed defeat on her face: my poor mother, already suffering from a maiming social inferiority complex, was now dealt another blow of shame. Mind you, I learned later from my younger sister, Susan, that Mum had had her suspicions that I might be pregnant but she had also kept silent, I guess hoping against hope that it wasn't true.

The mother

Now that the worst was confirmed, though, what to do? Well, obviously, the first priority was that no one could know; this thing must be hidden. In other words, I must be hidden, and before it was altogether too late. Here's where the beauty of the remote 'eastern states' came into play: my parents could send me away to the far country – Melbourne, to be precise.

Family energies were harnessed to achieve the success of the cover-up plan and there was much to organise: my urgent departure for Melbourne, ostensibly to take up an unspecified and unlikely offer of employment; the matters of accommodation, doctor, hospital – and the arrangements for the adoption of the baby, already established as a given, an inevitability.

Why was it assumed, by me as well, that I could not actually keep the baby and care for it? What was wrong with me?! I suppose parental and social pressure combined with an immature selfishness and the desire on my part to continue my youthful hopes and dreams as I had always imagined them – which did not include being an unmarried mother. Tim, at twenty, certainly was neither ready nor willing to be a father. He felt that his own adult life had barely started. His personal ambitions were half-formed but enticing, and he didn't want his wings clipped just as they were unfolding; and neither did I. I had completed my Bachelor of Arts degree at the end of 1964 and I wanted to travel, to have adventures – and I did not want to lose Tim, which, wrongly or rightly, I thought I definitely would if I kept the baby. I see now that it was a sad and selfish choice, but that is who I was then.

So it was that I sort of sleepwalked my way through the plan. I caught the plane to Melbourne (not a moment too soon as far as concealment of the pregnancy went), and, as arranged, was billeted with a kind single-mother nurse in Doncaster, an outer suburb of Melbourne. Living with a stranger in a strange town, I became further alienated from reality. Life in a bubble.

Tim visited me once during this period and stayed for about a week. We were sort of 'together' but whatever conflicting thoughts and emotions we may have had, we both remained committed to the plan of adoption. As to where our relationship might go afterwards, we didn't really discuss it – we were like children ourselves, rather than serious, responsible adults.

About two weeks before my due date, I moved down to a city hotel to be closer to the hospital. My mother came over to be with me, which I appreciated, but the time was emotionally fraught. I have a memory of myself, nine months pregnant, hurrying along Bourke Street, tears streaming down my face. A young man from a Christian group reached out to me with compassion and said, 'Jesus loves you.' Some fifteen years later I would come to know this wonderful truth for myself, but at the time I shrank away from what seemed to be an embarrassing exposure of my needy humiliation.

In due course my waters broke, Mum called a taxi, and we arrived at St Andrew's Hospital. I retain a memory of the labour ward, coldly sterile and flooded in a lurid white light. People in masks administered strong medication, which took me into a shadow world where I was an actor in a drama, detached from myself. At the moment of delivery, I was given an even stronger anaesthetic that knocked me out completely. Blackout. When I woke, all was how it should be: Robin was no longer pregnant. Nor was Robin a mother. The plan had worked most efficiently.

There were small cracks in the coffin lid of denial, though. I remember sitting like a stone statue with my mother in the doctor's office as he went through the final paperwork for the adoption. First, the birth certificate: I was told that my name would be recorded but the father's name would be left blank, as was common practice if the relinquishing mother was unmarried. The doctor then asked me to give the baby a name for the birth certificate. I was not prepared for this, as it had never been discussed, and, as I dumbly and numbly hesitated, he suggested, 'What about Helen?'

A tiny shoot of ownership pushed through my façade and I said, 'No. Florence.' It was my mother's name and seemed to make the baby one of us – no one in the family had ever been called Helen. I glanced at my mother and saw tears in her eyes. Then it came to signing the adoption consent form, which would 'permanently and totally' deprive me of my 'parental rights', and the crack widened, allowing my own tears to leak through. But the deal was done, the die was cast.

I returned to Perth, where I resumed my life and my relationship with Tim, and buried the whole experience deep within my subconscious. In general, I tend to be a bit of a blabbermouth, not the soul of discretion, but the fact that I had adopted out a child was my one dark secret. It lay largely undisturbed for twenty-four years.

The child

Susannah

I can't remember being told that I was adopted: it was just something I always knew, part of our family story. Mum and Dad had had one little girl who died just hours after her birth, then came my brother, Duncan, and then, tragically, another little girl who was stillborn. Then came me in 1965 and, two years later, my sister Sophie.

The story of my adoption went something like this: The woman who had you loved you very much but she couldn't keep you, so she made sure you went to a family that could look after you and love you. Mummy and Daddy waited and waited for you and were so excited when we were called to come and get you. We walked down the hospital corridor and there you were – our beautiful daughter.

The nurses at the hospital had called me Joan Sutherland. This had always been told as a funny story, but the reason for the name was anything but amusing: I cried and screamed so much, and so loudly, they thought I had the lungs of an opera singer. And, apparently, I kept on crying when I was taken home. I wouldn't take the bottle, I threw up the formula when I finally did drink, and I fought everything. Mum, still grieving the loss of two daughters, cried with me.

Besides my crying, there was a further brake on our early bonding attempts. The adoption laws at the time allowed the birth mother a cooling-off period of thirty days, meaning she could change her mind and reclaim her baby. When I was an adult with kids of my own, Mum and I talked about this. She told me how hard she found it, grieving her first two daughters and desperately trying to bond with her third as I screamed and kicked and fought her – all the time fearing that this one, too, might be taken from her. Unimaginable.

And Mum and Dad would tell me later how the angry baby became an angry toddler, obsessed with whose tummy I came out of and cross with Duncan, because he came out of Mummy's and I didn't. I cringed when Dad told me the story of how I punched a pregnant friend of theirs in her belly (thankfully without harm), declaring to Mum that I wanted to come out of her tummy. I recall none of this, nor do I remember asking Mum, at around two-and-a-half, if she was my mother. Mum told the story this way.

'You looked at me with those intense eyes, waiting for an answer. I loved you very much but was battling my own fears that I was not worthy to be your mother. I took a deep breath and said, "Yes. I am your mother." You flew across the room and into my arms and hugged me.'

I wish my head could remember that moment, but I'm sure my heart does. I think it must have been the moment Mum and I locked in for life.

Over a childhood we both healed and wrangled our relationship and she became, as mothers do, the most important person in my life. I grew up in a family, my family, where I felt unconditionally loved and wanted. My parents gave me countless opportunities and endless support. My dad and I shared a love of verbal jousting, and I loved to read and write, just like both my parents did. Duncan and Sophie, my brother and sister, were my companions and combatants in the same measure they are in all families, and I loved them. I may not have looked like anyone else in the family, but that happens, right? It didn't matter. I was healed and I was home.

And as I got older, the story of my birth, the reason I didn't look like the rest of my family, became simply a technical detail that I would, at times, have to explain to people.

'Why don't you look like your mum?' curious school friends would ask.

'Because I'm adopted,' I would reply with an assured confidence, as if I was explaining that the sky is blue.

'So, who's your real mother, then?' they would continue.

'Mum's my real mum.'

'No, your *real* one,' they would press. 'The one who *had* you.'

'Oh, she's not my mum. She was just my birth mother, the one who delivered me,' I would reply, implying some kind of biological postal system.

The names people play. No story here, nothing to see, nothing to tell. No problem. The first ten days of my life was summed up in my Year 3 story, 'The Adventures of Me'.

I was born on the 14th of July 1965. My mother who had me could not keep me. So Mrs G. McFarlane adopted me a few days after my birth.

My sense of self, of home, the strength of my connection with Mum, was so locked in, it survived even direct challenges. Once, when I was in Year 3, I had forgotten my school lunch and Mum brought it to me in my classroom. I must have been talking to my classmates about my adoption recently because, as Mum approached the classroom, one girl cried out, 'Don't take your lunch from her! She's not your real mother!'

But she was. She bloody was, and I went and took my lunch to prove it. I had a mum and a dad and a family who loved me and whom I loved. End of story. Everyone else could deal with it.

The tummy aches and tantrums of my toddlerdom faded, healed by Mum and Dad's patient, constant love, and I grew up. And I forgot all about the other mother who couldn't keep me.

II

FALSE START

Prelude

Robin

In 1966 Tim left for Europe and I followed him in the spring of 1967, looking forward to the carefree adventures we both had wanted. The fact that we had adopted out a child was consigned to some never-to-be-opened file in the memory bank of the mind. We went on a hitchhiking trip together, travelling south from Paris, through France and Spain to Morocco before returning to London. Soon after our return, Tim secured a one-year contract as a drama lecturer at a college in Ohio. He left and I remained at my London post as a salesgirl on the men's pyjamas counter of Marks & Spencer until a drunken late-night phone call from America rescued me with a marriage proposal from Tim. I flew to New York and we were married in the City Hall in December 1967.

After a year in Ohio, we returned to Australia and, in 1969, Tim got a job with the drama department of Flinders University in Adelaide, and I taught English at a high school. It was at this stage of our life that the prevailing hippie culture with its philosophy of freedom from the bonds of bourgeois morality – which included monogamy – began to undermine our marriage. 'Enlightenment' through the use of mind-altering drugs didn't exactly help either. In fact, Tim became more and more depressed and creatively jammed. In December 1972 Anna was born and, shortly after, we moved to Melbourne where Tim, abandoning academia, had joined the Pram Factory Drama Cooperative. That we had returned to the place where I had given up my first baby was a fact I must have registered but pushed down and away.

Although there were good people and good things in our life in Melbourne, our lifestyle and marriage deteriorated and, with fewer and fewer moral boundaries, we got ourselves into a big mess. Our romantic and sexual entanglement with another couple – Andy and Charmayne – engulfed us all in confusion, jealousy, anger and grief. Matilda was born to Tim and me in 1977 amid emotional chaos, and soon after, Tim moved out to be with Charmayne, whom he later married. Andy wanted to be with me.

By Anna's sixth birthday – 6 December 1978 – it seemed the storm winds had died down and the four of us found peace and reconciliation with each other. The girls and I left with Andy to go on a beach holiday together and, on 14 December, Andy drowned.

Nineteen seventy-nine was a year of intense pain and attempts to ease that pain in all sorts of wrong ways, especially promiscuity. I was desperately trying to replace love lost, but of course it doesn't work that way.

Towards the end of the year, I moved with Anna and Matilda into a dear little cottage in Dryburgh Street, North Melbourne. I was able to buy it thanks to money left to me by Andy, and it provided a safe and secure haven where emotional healing could begin. Sometime in 1980, I found myself with a new quest – not for love and happiness, but for truth. I wanted to know the answer to that old question: 'what is the meaning of life?' That search unexpectedly led me to Jesus Christ and in January 1981 I became a Christian.

I was born again in my spirit, but it took some time for the new life on the inside of me to grow and gradually change the rest of me – my thinking, and my old ways of doing things. For a while, I was a strange sort of hybrid, mutating from one thing to another, which was confusing to me and to others. It was especially perplexing to Graeme, whom I met on the cusp of my transformation; I slept with him and became pregnant. If I had not yet grasped God's thinking with regard to casual sex, the Holy Spirit did arrest me on the matter of abortion – and I am so glad He did, because in June 1982, I gave birth to my fourth daughter, Marian, a joy to both me and her father. Graeme and I did not stay together, but we have remained friends and family, as have Tim and Charmayne and their children, Finn and Billie.

Waking up

Robin

T.S. Eliot wrote: 'April is the cruellest month, breeding/ Lilacs out of the dead land . . .'

Resurrection is costly; it's easier sometimes to stay dead, sleeping or numb, rather than feel the quickening pain of pins and needles that signal the return of blood flow and the consequent call to feel and live again. But then, you never get to enjoy the beauty of the lilacs.

In the Spring of 1989, God, obviously with lilacs in His sight, decided it was time to wake me up regarding the birth and adoption of my baby in 1965 – a matter that was never discussed and I thought was well and truly dead and buried.

It was a strange week in October when I first started thinking about it again. After my initial out-of-the-blue thought, every day brought a reminder – like an alarm clock that refuses to let you lapse back to sleep. God was on my case! I turned on the radio – a talk about adoption; I opened a newspaper – an article on adoption; a lady came to stay with me from interstate as a billet for a conference – she had a personal story to tell me about adoption. *Okay, God,* I thought, *I get it!*

The conviction came to me that firstly, there was no place in my new life for deep, dark secrets and secondly, that I wanted (heart pounding at the thought) to try to reconnect with the daughter I had given away.

The first step in bringing everything up into the light was to tell my three other daughters, Anna, then aged seventeen, Matilda, twelve and Marian, seven. I was terrified. What would they think of me, a mother who gave away her child? Would they recoil from me as from a monster? Would they lose all trust in me?

Their reaction in fact was beautiful: no judgment, just mercy and compassion and excitement over the fact that they had another sister somewhere whom, unanimously, they wanted to meet.

The next step was to contact the Department of Community Services and initiate the search for my daughter. I was required to go into the city offices for an interview and counselling, and when I got there I found many others there for the same reason: the desire to reunite. Parents seeking children, children seeking parents.

I gained some information about my daughter too: she was no longer called Florence, but Susannah; she lived in Hawthorn, Melbourne; her father taught English at university, her mother was a librarian. I was told, thanks to recent changes to the Adoption Law, that I was allowed to write Susannah a letter, which the department would pass on to her, if she was willing to accept it.

I wrote a letter.

Do not disturb

Susannah

While I believed that I had accepted my adoption as something that just was, that didn't need to be discussed, over the years many friends found it endlessly interesting. People continued to comment; my birth and adoption fascinated them, if not me, and it was regular dinner-party fodder. 'Aren't you curious?' 'Wouldn't you want to meet her?' 'What if you have sisters and brothers?' 'Don't you just want to know?'

'No, I don't,' I would answer. 'I have my family and I love them – I don't have another one. I don't have another mother.'

Except I did.

And I was completely unprepared when she came looking for me.

I was twenty-three. I had finished uni (graduating with an utterly un-vocational Arts degree) and had recently returned from overseas (where I had roamed Europe avoiding thoughts of what job one got with an Arts degree) when finally, with Dad's help, I found a position with a publishing company. I had worked my way up from super-menial to menial and was now a publicist and loved it: I loved the work, I loved the industry, and it seemed I had fallen into the perfect place for me. I had also fallen in love with a very handsome Swedish boy whom I planned to visit in Sweden at the end of the year, so I had moved back home to live with Mum and Dad while I saved money for the overseas trip. So, I was in a good place, a happy and exciting place. And then, one afternoon I came home from work to a letter from the Department of Community Services.

Community Services Victoria
29 Coventry Street
South Melbourne 3205
Phone 695 3888

CSV

Department of Community Services
Government of Victoria, Australia

ref

contact

AT:MK
ADOPTION SECTION
TELEPHONE: 695 3888

22 August 1989

Susannah M. McFarlane

Dear Susannah,

I write in relation to a sensitive matter concerning your family background. I appreciate that you may not be aware of this matter. My intention is purely to inform you of the present situation rather than cause you any distress. The matter to which I refer is that of your adoption.

As you may be aware, there have recently been significant changes to Victoria's adoption laws. One of these changes is that the natural relatives of an adopted person may apply to this Department for current information about that person. The Department must then approach the adopted person who has complete discretion over the release of such information.

We have received such an application from your natural mother. Her decision to request information was taken after much thought and discussion with a Counsellor. She is most concerned not to disturb your family's privacy and acknowledges your complete discretion in this matter. In making this application she is also happy to provide any background information which may be of interest to you.

I would like to discuss this application with you. My telephone number is (03) 695 3888.

I would like to assure you that the law gives full protection to your identity and whereabouts. Enclosed is a leaflet which sets out the main provisions of the new adoption laws.

The Adoption Information Service is also available to your adoptive parents should they at any time wish to talk to a Counsellor.

I look forward to hearing from you.

Yours sincerely,

COUNSELLOR
ADOPTION INFORMATION SERVICE

Encl.

There was supposed to be a band around the letter that warned it contained information of a deeply personal nature and that the letter might be best opened in private. The band was actually inside the deeply personal letter, which I found only after I had opened it – not a good start. And it did not get any better.

My 'natural mother'? My birth mother, right? I was already offside. Mum was my natural mother and she would be home from work soon. She would know what to do.

She'd barely made it through the front door when I handed her the letter and I can still remember her face when she saw what it was. It kind of crumpled and I could see her fighting to not look upset. 'Oh,' she said, struggling to keep her voice even, 'I did wonder if this day might come. Let me read it and then let's talk.'

She took the letter into her study and stayed in there some time: when she came out she was calmer but still tense. Then Dad arrived home from work and we all talked about what to do next. 'Well,' said Mum. 'You should call the counsellor. See what she wants.'

I don't remember what else happened that evening but I called the counsellor the next day from work and I do remember that call – it was awful.

The counsellor said I must be very excited.

I said I wasn't.

She carried on – my mother wanted to meet me.

I told her that I didn't want to meet my birth mother.

The counsellor became a little cross at me – why would I not want to meet 'my mother'?

I told her I had just left 'my mother' at home.

'You mean your adoptive mother,' she said, a little testily.

Now I was getting cross too. 'No. I mean my mother.'

'Your mother wants to meet you. Are you really telling me that you don't want to meet your real mother?'

But I had had years of experience in explaining to people who my real mother was, and this counsellor was no match for me.

'She is not my mother,' I said.

There was a change of tack on the other end of the phone.

'Will you accept a letter?'

'Yes, I'll accept a letter – but I can't meet her. Please understand that I can't meet her.'

So, I waited for a letter.

Robin's first letter

Susannah

I don't have the first letter Robin sent. I don't know what happened to it, but it must have got lost. I kept nothing about Robin's contact, but after Mum died I discovered that she had kept a folder containing all the letters and notes about my adoption. But this letter wasn't there and Mum is no longer here to ask.

In a funny way, part of me is glad it's lost.

Robin

This is what I remember writing.

I expressed my hope that this letter would not distress Susannah, and I was at pains to say that I in no way wanted to challenge or intrude upon the relationship she had with her adoptive mother, who had earned and fulfilled that title in reality.

I wanted to be completely honest and put all my cards on the table. I confessed to her that I had gone on to marry Tim, her father, and that she had two full sisters, Anna and Matilda, and one half-sister, Marian, all of whom would love to know her.

I told her I had become a Christian. I asked her to forgive me for having given her up. I said I would love to meet her if she wanted to.

I waited for her reply. I waited a long time.

The letter I dreaded

Susannah

Mum and Dad were on an overseas holiday at the time I received the letter from Robin. I waited until they got home before I answered it.

I remember reading the letter, but not everything in it. I remember Robin saying she was sorry, all the more so because after having me, she went on to stay with my biological father. She also said that I had two full biological sisters and a half-sister. I don't remember how I felt, but I do remember thinking it strange that she called her daughters my sisters. And strange that she seemed to think we would be meeting. She wanted my forgiveness; my 'sisters' wanted to meet me.

But I already had a family and most of all I had Mum and Dad, who had loved me and looked after me all my life and whom I loved wholeheartedly. Seeing Mum's face when I showed her the letter from Community Services had already told me what I needed to do. I would not risk breaking my mother's heart: I wouldn't, couldn't, meet my birth mother.

And how could I, anyway? I couldn't meet Robin as my mother, yet I couldn't meet her as anything else either. So, I couldn't meet her at all.

But I could certainly forgive her and tell her that it was okay, that it had all worked out really well. And perhaps she could tell me any genetic medical history? I was tired of not being able to fill out medical forms, tired of writing 'unknown' in every single box about my 'family' history and tired of enduring nurses' sympathetic looks. And, sometimes I worried: Did cancer run rampant in my biological ancestry or were there other horrible afflictions waiting to genetically pounce? Would it be okay to ask her about that?

I wanted to say to her: *I have a wonderful life, I am loved and love, and I am happy – I hope you are too. I forgive you. Can we leave it at that? But, actually, can you also please let me know my medical history?* Was that a fair letter to write?

I thought it was, and Mum and Dad thought it was too, so I sat down at the long dinner table in our back room and tried to write that letter. I tried to be honest, I tried to be open, and I tried to make everything okay. I don't remember feeling upset, I don't remember feeling anything other than worried that I would upset Mum and Dad, who waited for me to show them my draft.

Robin had put her address on her letter to me but I didn't do that on mine. I remember Mum saying, 'Don't name the college, don't name the uni, don't say where you work – I could find you if I had that information.' This was pre-Internet of course, pre-Google; if you were going to be found you had to want to be.

And I didn't.

The letter I dreaded

10 December 1989

Dear Robin

This is indeed an amazing letter to write and, to be honest, one which I hoped I would never have to. I would like to apologise for the delay in my reply but I wanted to wait until my parents returned from overseas — I hope this delay did not cause you any distress.

What to say to you — I really don't know. However the most important thing for you to know is that there is absolutely nothing for me to forgive you for. What must have been a truly awful time for you has resulted in a terrifically happy life for me. I have two great parents and a brother and a sister and, having completed a tertiary degree three years ago, a fun job as a publicist. I also have a Swedish boyfriend who I'm going to spend Christmas with in Sweden before he comes out to live here.

I don't know if this is of interest to you but these seemingly minor bits of

information add up to the fact that I am well, happy and with family and friends who I love and who love me.

It is perhaps partly because of this that I cannot meet you and your family. It is also because I can't see on what level such a meeting could occur — I could not meet you as potential friend and yet I cannot meet you as my mother. I have a mother and I suppose it is also because of my great love for her that I feel we should not meet.

I am sincerely sorry if my decision upsets you in any way but perhaps it may also finally erase a question mark in both our minds — I certainly hope you feel no guilt.

In the light of what I have just written, my request now seems incredibly selfish but I would like to know if there is any abnormal medical history in your family. I hope this question

is not a distressing one and I only ask it because at the moment I cannot fill out much of a hospital's admission form ie history of heart disease, strokes etc. My main concern is not so much for myself any more but for that of any children I may have or carry, unaware of any possible genetic problems I may pass on to them.

I know this seems harsh and scientific (particularly since I cannot help you in what you want) but I would be grateful if you could pass any such information to me via community services.

Robin — I don't know how to finish this letter except to say that I am sorry and that I sincerely hope you and your family have long and happy lives and that you especially might now have more peace of mind.

With all good wishes

Susannah

'With all good wishes . . .'

Robin

So. What did I think when I finally received Susannah's letter? How did I feel?

There was no ambiguity about her decision to have no contact with me. Certainly, I felt the blow and disappointment of rejection, but I was in no way offended. How could I be? I understood where she was coming from, and I took satisfaction in the fact that at least I had, albeit in a very superficial way, reversed the roles: now I wanted her, but this time she could reject me. It felt better that way.

I found it a 'young' letter; it reminded me of myself at that age – the age I was when I gave birth to her, in fact. It was formal and sort of frozen, perfectly polite and controlled, showing no emotion. She was the adult ministering to me, assuring me there was nothing to forgive, expressing solicitude over my wellbeing. She described her perfect and complete life and declared her total loyalty to her adoptive mother and family. I did not doubt the truth of that happiness and love, but I still sensed something behind the façade of mature efficiency: the naivety and insecurity of a child. My heart went out to her.

So then, of course, I had to write back to her, assuring her of the acceptability of her letter, the validity of her loyalty to her adoptive mother, and my unconditional, albeit background, love for her as the child I birthed. No strings attached.

I wrote back:

17 December 1989
Dear Susannah
Thank you for replying to my letter. I very much appreciate your sharing the broad details of your life with me. I am so glad that you are well, happy and loved.

Don't think that I had the slightest thought of taking any of your mother's place. I know very well that it's the daily working, caring and loving that makes a mother or father. I am very grateful that your mother was there for you.

Thank you for saying that you don't hold the past against me.

Of course I won't initiate any further contact with you but I repeat that you and your family would always be welcome should you decide to contact me in the future.

There are no abnormalities in the family history – quite healthy on both sides – so you can be reassured on that score.

Also be at peace as far as I am concerned. I am happy and secure and you certainly need feel no responsibility or anxiety on my behalf. Just accept me as someone else who <u>really cares</u> about you in the background. It never hurts to have a bit more love, does it?
God bless you, Susannah.
With love,
Robin

And that was that. I was sad when I learned that only a very small percentage of adoptees don't want contact with their birth mother. Susannah and I were in that percentage.

I was also sad telling Anna, Matilda and Marian that there was no big sister on the horizon just yet. However, they didn't forget her, and I'm sure they each thought about her and imagined what it would be like if they ever did actually get to meet her. Although we had no information about her physical appearance, Matilda in particular confessed to being often on the lookout – in the city, on trams, at the Victoria Market – for a dark-haired young woman with an uncanny resemblance to herself.

So, Susannah became a sort of phantom member of our family: always there in the background of our consciousness like a will-o-the-wisp, not entirely relinquished, still wistfully hoped for and sought.

Closing the door

Susannah

I remember thinking it was a nice letter from Robin, especially the bit about 'someone who really cares about you in the background', but I don't remember thinking much about it again. It was just a footnote to the dinner-party topic, a rounding-off of the story of why I didn't look like my mum and dad.

And, over time, I even forgot Robin's name.

Yet every now and then I would wonder – and wander. I did remember the street the letter was written from – Dryburgh Street, North Melbourne – and every now and then I would drive down it, sunglasses on. I'm not sure what I was expecting – perhaps three younger girls who looked like me walking down the street?

But I never saw anyone, let alone anyone who looked like me. And in later years when I would drive down again, those three girls wouldn't even have been living there anymore.

She was 'happy and secure' and so was I. We had all moved on.

III

OPENING LINES

Something stirs

Susannah

Life had been very good to my family and me for a long time. Oskar, the very handsome Swedish boy, and I went on to marry in 1993, and in 1996 we moved to London, where we lived for seven years. I had a dream job in publishing and we had had our two kids, Edvard and Emma, there. We enjoyed idyllic summers with family in Sweden and regular trips home to Australia. By 2002, though, we wanted to settle somewhere, to put down roots: I wanted to be closer to Mum and Dad as they aged, Oskar wanted to plant trees he would see grow, and we wanted our move to house number thirteen to be the last, at least for a while. So, in October, we came back to Melbourne. I started a publishing partnership, the kids started school, Oskar found a job and we all found a new home and a dog, Bill, to go with it. Life was good, very good. We felt blessed.

But then in 2008, things soured: Duncan's wife, my sister-in-law, Miffy, died suddenly and I had to leave a business I had co-founded. Then, in 2009, Mum was diagnosed with a rare and untreatable cancer, and my daughter became very unwell. So many things that had been solid were shaken and the whole family struggled to cope. Ultimately my enforced break from publishing was a blessing, though: I was able to travel to the UK to help my brother, and, then later, spend time with my daughter and with Mum as she first negotiated and then conceded to her illness.

I still remember the moment, in a cafe in Hawthorn where we met regularly, when Mum told me that there was no cure for the cancer and that it would move quickly. I had gone to meet her planning to tell her about some problem I was having, wanting her to help sort me out as she so often did, but, hearing her awful news, I didn't raise it. Indeed, in that moment I realised, decided, that after her nearly fifty years of love and care for me, it was my turn to care for Mum, to put her first, just as she had done for me countless times.

It was both excruciatingly sad and a wonderful privilege to be able, with Dad and Sophie, to help care for Mum as she prepared to die. In the shadow of the tragic death of my sister-in-law, Mum was determined to take away the fear, to show the family a 'good death', after a long life, well lived and loved. We all tried our best to embrace her plan but, of course, the certain knowledge of the impending loss hung heavy.

In her final weeks in October 2011, we each managed to have a special moment with Mum as she lapsed in and out of consciousness. Mine was on a beautiful sun-drenched spring morning. I had arrived at the hospice early – around 7am – to miss the morning cross-town traffic and to steal some time alone with Mum. We all knew the end was coming and, while we weren't ready, Mum was – almost too ready at times. I came into her room, kissed her and sat by her bed, taking her hand.

'Morning, Mum.'

'Hello, darling, am I dead yet?'

'No, Mum, not yet.'

'Oh. Soon?'

'Yes, Mum, soon.'

'And, Suse, do you think it will be okay?'

'Yes, it will be okay, Mum, it will be completely okay.'

'That's good. And …'

'Yes, Mum?'

'Did I do a good job as your mother?'

This question broke me.

'Yes, Mum, you did a wonderful job. I've been so lucky to have you. I love you, Mum.'

'That's good, darling. Take your best kiss now.'

And I did. It was the last fully conscious time I had with my mum, who died on the nineteenth of October.

Over the next three years, the family slowly recalibrated without its lynchpin. I worked out that it took perhaps seven friends to do the same job Mum had done for me, and with the illnesses of both my kids at times threatening to pull me under, I missed her terribly. Mum would have known what to do and I often didn't. It was all getting a bit much.

Early 2014

Robin

I had an interesting talk with Marian and her partner, Felix, this evening. Not sure how it began but we started talking about Susannah and whether I should make another attempt at contact.

I've been thinking about this for a while now, but I'm still unsure and don't want to impose. Both Marian and Felix are enthusiastically positive – they definitely think I should. Things are very different now – Susannah would be much older (forty-nine!), and very possibly with children of her own, giving her a new perspective.

But then, she could contact me if she wanted to, so presumably she doesn't. Maybe she's not alive? What an awful thought.

Is there anything to lose by trying, though? She can only refuse again. But it's her life and not my right to harass or upset her or cause distress. However, I suspect from the feeling of excitement beginning to stir inside me that these thoughts of moderating caution are perfunctory, tokenistic.

Because in my heart I know already – I'm going to make the move!

I contact the Department of Community Services and ask them to send me the relevant forms to apply for contact with my daughter.

Susannah

Exhausted and in need of a break after a particularly difficult time juggling writing deadlines and family issues, I take myself off for five days at Gwinganna Lifestyle Retreat in Queensland. One of the programs on offer is called The Journey, a guided visualisation of self-discovery. I would normally run from this sort of thing; I am against 'journeys' because so many people (would-be TV chefs and DIY-ers particularly) are having them – and so often – that they are becoming meaningless. But this time I put aside my scepticism: I am here to recover and recharge after a gruelling twelve months. I am up for anything.

And so, I give myself over to the process, and at one point I find myself talking to Mum, telling her what has been happening and telling her that I love her. I cry a lot. Then, all of a sudden, I am in my own delivery ward telling my birth mother I love her. I cry even more.

What the? Where did that come from? And what did it mean?

I have no idea, but I leave the session, have a bath, go to bed exhausted and sleep for twelve hours. Then I go on with the rest of the retreat and return to Melbourne a few days later, rested and relaxed.

I don't remember specifically reflecting on my 'conversations' with my two mothers, but then, a few weeks later, I have the thought that I want to write a better, kinder letter to my birth mother. If she is still alive, I want her to know that – having now had children myself – I feel for her and her decision and I want to apologise for what was perhaps an uncaring letter of rejection in 1989. That is the message of my 'journey', I reckon: to resolve things, to make things right.

Robin

Well, praise God, I'm still alive. Two weeks ago, I had just dropped my two grandchildren, Ada and Aziza, off at school and was driving home with their pug dog, Archie, sitting beside me in the front passenger seat. I was turning right at an intersection close to home when I literally didn't know what hit me. There was a huge crashing sound and I found myself falling forward and to the side before everything stopped moving. The driver of the other vehicle, hidden by cars stopped at the lights, had sped through the red light, hitting me as I completed my right turn.

Finding myself all in one piece, I undid my seatbelt and looked to see where Archie was. Amazingly, he was exactly as he had been: peacefully perched on the seat looking ahead, not a hair out of place, and yet he was on the side that received the full impact.

At the time, I had no feelings of being hurt except for soreness in my chest. Now, two weeks later, all my left side has turned black with bruising. It is more painful, but not excessively, and X-rays and ultrasounds have revealed only temporary soft-tissue damage.

How Archie spent that moment of collision remains a mystery. Was he flung against me and then bounced back again? I certainly have no recollection of such a thing and it seems unlikely, given his air of serenity. Did angels lift him out of harm's way for that brief moment and then return him to his seat? I find this a more plausible scenario. My car is a write-off, but I (and Archie) survived: God has future plans for me.

Closing and opening

Robin

I'm sitting in front of my computer, staring at the image of a mature woman with blonde curly hair, trying to compute the fact that this woman is, in fact, my child, my baby; I'm struggling to close the reality gap.

It is thanks to my niece, Florence (named, almost incredibly, without reference to either my mother or to the fact that this was the name that was put on Susannah's original birth certificate), that I have gained access to the considerable amount of online information about Susannah. On hearing of my intention to try to re-contact her, Florence, with all the zeal and technical skill of her generation, went into full sleuth/research mode and unearthed her quarry. This was the text she sent her mother, my sister, Susan:

> Would Robin think I was snooping if I was looking for Susannah on Google? I don't want to whip something up for her that I shouldn't but there is a chance I have found her, Susannah McFarlane, a children's author.

She has indeed found her – and we are all excited!

Her task was made easier by the fact that Susannah has quite a public profile, because she is a successful author of children's books! I am impressed. I am proud. I am happy for her.

I continue to stare at the photo, recognising with (perhaps illogical) wonderment the genetic connections. I see her paternal grandmother, Janet; my older sister, Pam; myself.

There is another picture of her sitting around a table with other writers, as part of a panel interview. There is something vulnerable about her in the photo, a little insecure? The way she holds her arm in particular reminds me of a child. I latch on to this thought because it seems to offer a way back, past the competent, successful adult to the never-seen baby that was mine. It touches my heart, and that's what I'm looking for – a heart connection.

Then I discover the transcript of another interview with Susannah in which she is asked biographical questions. Her answer to one of these stops me in my tracks. That little new shoot of hopeful anticipation I had felt deep within me tentatively reaching towards the surface is suddenly squashed back down. Quenched.

The interviewer asks her where she got her gift and love of writing, and Susannah replies, 'My father's an English teacher and writer, and my mum was a librarian and a poet. I guess it's in the blood.'

That's not her blood – but it seems she wants it to be. She doesn't want to know about her birth parentage. It's as I feared: she is still where she was when I wrote to her twenty-five years ago: she has a wonderful family and mother and she doesn't need another one, thank you very much.

How dare I disturb her chosen reality? It's not my right. She owes me nothing. I gave her away.

Is that it then, Lord? I thought you were doing something.

I feel disappointment, like a tangible substance, seeping through my bloodstream, sparing no crack or crevice where hope might still be hiding.

Defeated, I take the application forms I received from the Department of Community Services and put them in a drawer.

I close the drawer.

Susannah, 16 June

I open my email and write to FIND, the Family Information Networks and Discovery, Department of Human Services.

> As we discussed, my birth mother made contact with me in the late 1980s. After an exchange of letters, there was no further contact, as I felt unable to proceed beyond those letters. I would now, if possible, like to make contact again. As requested, I have attached a PDF of my driver's licence. Do let me know what I need to do next.

23 June

I've been assigned a caseworker named Maddy. So, now I'm a case? Excellent. I fill out the application form to obtain my adoption records. Maddy tells me it could take six to eight weeks for the records to arrive. I determine to forget about it until she contacts me again. And, on the whole, I do. I tell Oskar and the kids but no-one else in my family – there's no need. I have plenty of other things going on: there is a book deadline to meet, Oskar is starting a new business and my son is now halfway through VCE. It's a crazy year.

19 August

Maddy calls. The records have arrived but to get them I need to attend a Section 87 interview. Really? Can't they just confirm if she is alive and I can send the letter? Apparently not. An email from FIND elaborates.

> Depending on what you'd like to discuss we will go over the records located but also use it as an opportunity to talk about your thoughts and ideas for contact again with Robin.

People find the interviews useful in preparation for contact and fleshing out their expectations around relationship building.

Robin. Yes, that was her name. I remember now. But I don't have any expectations around relationship building. I am not planning to build a relationship. I just want to write a better letter.

25 August

I open the blue ring-binder folder.

I'm sitting with Maddy in a meeting room at FIND, a typically nondescript government office room. The blue folder contains all the held files and documents relating to the birth and adoption of Florence Leuba.

That's me. Was me. Is me?

My mind both races and freezes at the same time. I look at the birth certificate. My first one, the one that was sealed when I was adopted, the one that everyone was assured would never be released.

Baby – Florence Leuba
Mother – Robin Leuba
Father – [blank]

I can't really take it in. Maddy asks if I want to look through the folder with her. 'It's fine,' I say. 'I'll just take it home and maybe look then.' But Maddy is persistent. (Looking back I realise she'd probably seen this reaction before.) She says she needs to sign a form saying that I have read the contents of the folder. I don't want to get her into trouble on my account, so I concede – more out of politeness than interest.

So, we head off through the folder. There is a lot of legal stuff 'in the matter of Florence Leuba', but there are also handwritten letters: from Robin's mother to the social worker in Melbourne, the one who was going to make it all go away; then Robin's letter to the same; and later again, when she writes to confirm she will give up 'the baby'. Even that I skim read. *Oh, right*, I think but then I move on, dream-like, barely connecting that I'm that baby.

The only time I snap to and my heart pulls is when I see the letter Mum wrote to the social worker inviting her to a party to celebrate my becoming part of the family; it's been a while since I have seen Mum's distinctive handwriting and signature and it makes me sad. I miss her a lot.

There's other stuff too: copies of my hospital crib card, Robin's bed card, my discharge form and then page after page of affidavits 'in the matter of Florence Leuba'. It all passes in a bit of a blur.

Every now and then Maddy asks how I am. 'Yes, fine, I'm fine,' I reply.

But she persists. 'What do you think about it all, Susannah?'

No idea, I think, but I suspect Maddy thinks I should try a bit harder.

'So, is she still alive?' I ask.

'Yes,' confirms Maddy.

'So, I can write the letter?' The letter, the kinder letter that will make things better and draw a line under things. Everything will be resolved. And that will be that.

'Yes.'

I ask Maddy if she will contact Robin to ask if she will accept a letter from me. Maddy says she will and tells me to take care. She's lovely to care so much, but I'm fine, completely fine. I sign the form to say I have read the folder, then I pick it up and drive home.

When I get home I put the folder on my desk in my study and go into the kitchen to make dinner. Oskar comes home and asks how it went. I think I reply it was fine, that it felt a bit weird but it was fine.

From my family there is mild interest at best: after all, the way I have told them about it, I am just writing a letter. I'm not going to meet her. How could it possibly affect them? And so we have dinner, and I recount the meeting with Maddy in the same amount of time as other people's news of the day. I tell them my name was Florence. There is a group grimace and Emma suggests Susannah is more me. I tell them my birth mother's name is Robin Leuba. They don't have a view on that. After dinner, Oskar and the kids settle down to a TV show, but instead of joining them I go back up to my desk.

And I Google Robin Leuba. Well, you would, wouldn't you?

There's not much there, but there is an address. I Google that and find a picture of her house – it's small and across the other side of the city in a suburb I've never heard of.

I come downstairs for a glass of wine and tell my family as I pass through the living room to the kitchen that I have just Googled Robin and that she lives in Hadfield. There is a slight lift of the head by Oskar and a query as to where Hadfield is. My glass of wine and I go back upstairs and I Google some more.

Next I find a book Robin wrote. A writer: that piques my curiosity. I Google on. Called *All Things New*, the book is a self-published memoir and, from the blurb on the publisher's website, it seems to be a Christian testimonial. The last chapter has also been posted on the site. Am I going to read it? Yes, of course. Why not? Just to see. I might just get another glass of wine before I do it, though.

I come downstairs again and tell the family, 'She seems to be a born-again Christian.' The head lifts are a little more pronounced this time. I think Oskar says something like, 'But it doesn't matter, does it? You're just writing a letter.'

'Exactly,' I say as I walk back up the stairs.

But already I can feel that something's happening. There's a slight tightening of my chest and a flushing of my cheeks. And as I read the chapter, the tightening tightens and my heart begins to pound. There's been a lot of drinking, a lot of sleeping with men, then she finds God, and there's still drinking and sleeping with men. She gets pregnant, thinks about an abortion but can't square that with her faith, so keeps the baby. I am not that baby.

My head spins a little. I don't think I want to know all this, whatever this is, and yet I do. Except now I can't find the other chapters. I Google on, ferociously looking for more of the book, but, being self-published, it's not available for sale anywhere. Determined to read the book, my Googling takes me to the website of the State Library, where all books are lodged. The book is there, available for loan. I join the library online, reserve the book and decide to go into the city after my meetings the next day to read it.

Urgency seems to have arisen in me. I don't quite understand it but I decide to go with it. I also decide not to give my family any more updates for a while.

Reading between the lines

Robin, 26 August

In the morning mail there is an official-looking envelope: 'Sensitive material inside: open in private.' What? I have no idea whom this letter could be from.

FIND. Haven't heard of it. I tear it open and read the words: 'Your daughter, Susannah …' then I almost black out. It seems Susannah has contacted the organisation and has expressed a wish to write to me. Would I accept a letter from her?

This is incredible! It is only a few months ago that I consigned my dream of reconnecting with my adopted-out daughter to the drawer of oblivion!

There is a number to ring and I go straight to the phone. 'May I speak to Maddy, please?' They tell me that she is currently in a meeting, so I ask if she could call me back as soon as she is available to do so. I think the girl on the end of the phone senses I am a little overwrought and possibly communicates this to Maddy, who rings back sooner than I had been led to expect. I tell Maddy I am *extremely* willing to receive a letter from Susannah.

Susannah, 26 August

My meetings over, I head off to the State Library, feeling both a little ninja-sleuth and a little sick in the stomach. The book is waiting for me on the collections shelf. As I pick it up, I'm not sure I want to read it anymore. What if I don't like what I read?

I find a chair. I get up and find another one. And then another one. Where does one sit to read such words, the story of your birth mother?

I get over myself and sit down again. I read the blurb and, as I suspected, feared, it is a Christian testimonial. I'm not a Christian. I meditate and am interested in Buddhism, but in a secular way: if I'm anything, I'm a humanist, believing in the human rather than the holy spirit. I believe everyone has a right to their own choice and I respect those choices, but I confess that anything that is too full-on, too evangelical, scares me. From the first pages it seems, to me, pretty full-on Christian and it makes the book, and Robin, feel very alien to me.

Nonetheless I press on. It seems to be the story of her life yet I'm not in it. I skim through to find the pages describing the time of her life where I would appear. I find them but not me – although I am possibly in this line:

Selfish egocentricity was ever the order of the day and of course hearts were broken – those of boyfriends, girlfriends, parents – the usual thing.

But otherwise I don't exist. I have been excised from her life. She's forgotten about me, so perhaps she doesn't need my letter, doesn't want it. This is her life and I am not in it, not even as a footnote – bundled up with all the other bad mistakes she made. Maybe it's just as well: we seem to have lived very different lives, what connection could we possibly have?

So, now I'm thinking that I should just stop here and not even write the letter. It's not such a good idea after all; it's better to leave it all alone.

27 August

Maddy rings. Robin is extremely keen to receive a letter. Oh. I guess I need to finish what I started.

Careful correspondence

Susannah, 1 September

So, I think this is what I wanted to say. This is a better letter. I write it on the weekend and send it off to Maddy on Monday to see what she thinks.

29 August 2014

Dear Robin

Thank you for accepting this letter. My hope is to write a 'better' letter than I think I did last time. If there is a benefit to being older, I hope it is in being a bit wiser and a lot kinder. I'm sorry this letter is not handwritten but this way it's legible . . .

Many things, besides the deterioration of my handwriting, have happened since that first letter but two, becoming a mother and losing my mother, have been the most significant and they have, perhaps inevitably, reminded my head and heart of you.

It was not until I carried and had children of my own that I could really begin to understand, to feel, what you might have gone through and I have since wondered, worried, that I was not mindful of your experience when I replied to your first letter.

Then, I didn't, couldn't, understand but now, at least I know how I would feel in your situation: the isolation of a confinement; the conflict you might have felt as a baby grew inside you; and, finally, the wrench of the birth and separation. It must have been awful.

The guardedness in my first letter sprung also from a desire to protect my mum, who feared she would lose me. In my determination to reassure her, I perhaps denied you things. Mum can't be hurt now and is, I hope, at peace. Between nature and nurture, I am what I am in many ways because of both of you and, so, if I can now add a little to your peace, I would like to do that.

I'm not sure what else to say and I certainly don't know where this letter might lead but I hope you see it as a good thing. Like last time, I am still unsure what we, a pair of significant strangers, do with each other but am willing, albeit nervously so, if you are, to have a different exchange this time around.

All best

Susannah

Email from Maddy to Susannah, 9.23am

Hi Susannah,

Thank you for sharing your letter with me. If there was anything to motivate me on a Monday morning it would absolutely have to be your touching, honest, generous letter.

I realise I'm not Robin, but I think it's perfect.

I like how you have described what has brought you to this point and acknowledged Robin's journey. What I really liked was that you named what you are – significant strangers. I think being clear about who you are creates those boundaries that you are hoping for.

I can't think of any feedback or suggestion other than my enthusiasm!

It is always difficult to know how the other party will respond. It's impossible to know. But I believe this letter is the start of a careful conversation. I think that is what you would like and I also think Robin will happily accept.

Let me know what you're thinking and do feel free to give me a buzz if you'd like to talk it through.

Email from Susannah to Maddy, 10.51am

Thanks Maddy, I'm pleased you think it's hitting the right note – I did want to be open but with boundaries. Let's send it off and see what happens

Email from Maddy to Susannah, 4.14pm

Hi Susannah,

Have just got off the phone to Robin and forwarded through your letter by email.

She will email back her response (to my email address) when she has one.

She sounded, and stated, that she was excited to receive your letter.

Hope you are feeling okay?

Am I feeling okay? No. I feel sick.

Robin, 1 September

I have just received the letter from Susannah.

It's a lovely, kind letter, but something is wrong. It's a letter of apology. She feels bad about her 1989 letter to me, fearing she had

52

been cold and had hurt me and not empathised with my trauma and pain.

'So, if I can now add a little to your peace, I would like to do that.'

Oh no! This is all the wrong way around. I am not the victim here, and it's not Susannah who owes me anything. She said in 1989 that she had 'absolutely nothing to forgive me for'. I knew then it wasn't true; she did, she does.

In my sealed-off selfishness, I wounded her deeply. Over the years, I have thought of her, prayed for her and about her, desired to connect with her. But I have not been living in trauma; I have not lacked peace. I cannot claim to be like those cases where the baby was taken away from the mother against her will; it was my decision. People may have told me I didn't really have a choice, but I did. And I chose me, not us.

This is serious: she has a false picture of me. What will she think of me when she is disillusioned as to my suffering (or lack thereof)? Is that the further ultimate rejection – that she really was not wanted?

Oh God! This is awful! The last thing I want to do is hurt her again, and I also don't want her to reject me or hate me. *Because I want her now.* But we cannot base our relationship (if we are to have one) on a lie. I won't be a fraud.

This is really scary. Will there be forgiveness, or not? How do I reply? I won't pretend anything, but maybe we don't have to brave the hugest challenges head-on just yet.

Susannah, 2 September

Email from Maddy to Susannah, 9.20am

Hi Susannah,

I have received a reply to your letter from Robin this morning.

Is it ok for me to forward it to this address?

Email from Susannah to Maddy, 9.25am

Wow, that was quick – yes please, forward.

Emailed Letter from Robin to Susannah, 9.28am

Dear Susannah,

It does feel rather surreal to be actually writing to you like this, but I am so glad to be doing so. Thank you for your letter.

A point that came up with Maddy seems quite telling: you wrote your first letter to me at pretty much the same age that I was when I gave birth to you, and now you have contacted me at roughly the same age I was when I contacted you! And I do feel we were quite parallel in our emotional development. As you say, age and experience changes us. But Susannah, just as in your first letter you said you had nothing to forgive me for, please don't think I found any fault with that letter; I totally understood where you were coming from.

Maybe Maddy also told you that I had only earlier this year thought to try and contact you again – forms are still sitting in a drawer – but then I thought it might still be an unwanted intrusion and imposition for you, so I didn't proceed. It's wonderful that you have taken this initiative – wherever it may, or may not, lead.

Should I feel guilty that I know quite a bit about you due to the younger generation's ability to search the Net? My niece, not even knowing your surname but a few salient facts, found you on the Internet. With a certain fear and trembling I followed her leads and have read about you and seen pictures of you. Of course, quite easy because you are famous! Really it is so fantastic to see what you have achieved; I am very impressed – and also deeply grateful to your parents for providing you with a foundation in life that

54

allowed you to develop your potential and talents. You are obviously also a superb mother.

You do look like your birth family, which is logical of course, but nonetheless sort of amazing to see, emotionally. (There are also some other interesting similarities!)

Susannah, please feel free to ask any questions you like. For my part, any contact is welcome.

Love, Robin

Susannah

I find it hard to concentrate as I read. My eyes blur and dart, my heart races and I feel sick, again. My tummy turns and my mouth dries. This is my birth mother. She's seen pictures of me? I look like them? What are those similarities? But hold on, stop, it's done now, isn't it? I've written my letter, she has replied saying it's all okay. So, that's all good, isn't it? Yet she seems to expect a reply: that wasn't really in the plan.

But I do write a reply and I ask for a photo. It's like I'm writing the letter but not really – I'm just watching as this other Susannah leads me further into whatever this thing is.

Email from Susannah to Robin, 10.48am

Hi Robin

Thank you for your reply. 'Surreal' is certainly a good word for this process: I am also working with 'weird' and my daughter, Emma, has gone with 'freaky'. She, about to turn 15 tomorrow, is very interested in this whole process and whether there will be any physical resemblances. Both kids look ridiculously like my husband's Swedish family but, of course, absolutely nothing like my side and so Emma, not so much Edvard, wonders.

And while we don't want any guilt, yes, it is unbalanced, and a little unfair, that I'm more Google-able than you! We did try but the internet seems low on Leubas. The only thing I could find was your book, *All Things New*, which I read with probably a similar fear and trembling as you trawled the internet. (I confess I was a little thrown when I didn't appear.)

So, if you're willing, I would like to see a photo of you, perhaps just you for now if that's ok as I think I need to keep things slow. And you have effectively piqued my curiosity with the 'interesting similarities' so if you want to elaborate, that would be great. I'm also happy to answer any questions you have, if I can.

Best
Susannah

Robin

Yes, the book. Two years ago, in 2013, I self-published a personal testimony about how I became a Christian. I deliberately made no mention of Susannah at the time, because I felt I could not possibly do so without her knowledge and consent. A family member had raised the question when I was writing it – how would Susannah feel about being expunged if she ever read it? I didn't think it would be a problem (but then I never do!). Now I see that it is. I have to explain.

I'm not sure how I feel about the 'Best' sign-off either. It sounds strange to my ears, quite cool and detached, in control …

Email from Robin to Susannah, 3.05pm

Dear Susannah,

Thanks for your quick reply. This is also ridiculously instant but I want to explain re my book. It will take me longer to send a photo as I am actually a technological idiot and will have to seek help as to how to send a photo via email. I have no idea how my story got on the Net and I was not pleased to discover that the publisher – without my permission – had put it on there.

Two reasons why you were not in it: firstly, I genuinely thought that to include that event without your consent would be a violation of your privacy and perhaps of a desire on your part to keep it unknown; secondly, it was by no means a complete autobiography – more a Christian testimony with a fairly narrow thematic thread. Maybe as a writer you can understand that angle of literary selection? But the first reason was the main one.

The 'interesting similarities' I referred to were just two 'small' things, I guess. Two of my daughter Anna's favourite things were 'The Enchanted Wood' and 'ABBA'. (Also Lady Di!! – but you probably didn't share that!) And your favourite word 'discombobulated' is I believe Tim's favourite word – which he introduced me to! Freaky?!

I would like to know about your sibling(s?): older? younger? I gather not also adopted. I will attempt the mission of sending a photo of myself.

Love, Robin

Susannah

I jump on the email and read it. Okay, I kind of get her explanation about the book, but I'm distracted by her confirmation that it's a Christian testimony – again, it alienates me. But there's the reference to ABBA, which is always a weak spot, and I soften. Then she mentions Tim, my birth father – I haven't even thought about him and now it seems we share a word preference? I can't work out if this is good or bad or something else. Probably discombobulating.

But now Emma is home from school and we have her fifteenth birthday to prepare for: presents to wrap, a real life to return to.

Watching our words

Susannah

Much later that night, with presents wrapped and a soon-to-be birthday girl asleep, my mind starts charging. I can't sleep. I toss and turn and so, rather than wake up Oskar, I get up and sit at my desk, reading Robin's letter again and again. And then I write one back. And this one feels strangely easy to write; I feel like I'm talking to someone I know.

Email from Susannah to Robin, 11.25pm

Hi Robin

Thank you for taking on the mission of a photo – now I see where I may have got my technical ineptitude from – at least you have a generational excuse!

I'm sorry about reading your book – it now feels like I've read someone's diary rather than a book meant for publication. That must feel weird for you, knowing I read that, perhaps knowing more about your life than you would choose me

to know? Sorry if it does. And thank you for explaining –
I completely understand.

There was more weirdness but in a much more amusing
way reading that your daughter also loved *The Enchanted
Wood* (the first book I remember really taking me away in my
imagination) and ABBA (who I absolutely adored, still do. I plan
to have 'Dancing Queen' played, slow beat, at my funeral).

Still on books, and the risk of it sounding like a speed-dating
question, I wonder what books you have on your bedside
table? I have *The 100 Year Old Man Who Climbed Out the
Window* (which I never finished), *Zen Mind, Beginner's Mind*
(I am a baby, baby Buddhist), *Three Cups of Tea* (about a
mountain climber who began building schools in Pakistan),
the new Murakami (which I am a little intimidated by) and
Cold Comfort Farm (which I just keep there because it makes
me laugh). I also have a collection of short stories, largely
chosen for their length (the shortest is a paragraph) for the
nights I have no attention span.

To your question, I have two siblings: a brother and sister. My
brother is older and my sister is younger. Unsurprisingly, I don't
look like anyone in my family. There is a photo taken of all of us
in a city street when I was about ten years old and it looks like
I have photo-bombed a lovely family of dark-haired people.

My brother is seriously academic, but in maths, so no one in the
family actually understands anything he does, and hasn't since
about 1980. When we were younger we were often adversaries,
as siblings can be, framing and blaming each other as we
vied for parental attention. I often felt I needed protection from
Duncan and his schemes – like practising his kung fu on me!
Yet, when we both went to the same university and college, he
became my protector, and while I am pretty sure he didn't use
his latent kung fu skills on anyone, he cleared a path for me,

looked after me. One of my favourite photos of the two of us together shows me standing behind him, my head peering over his shoulder. His elbow is raised and it might be a little unclear whether he is shielding or preparing to strike me if it were not for Duncan's soft face and lovely smile. For someone who broke no rules when he was at home – unhelpful for the child following – he broke quite a few later and we broke some together – just as you should when you are young.

He now lives in the UK, with his own research lab at Cambridge University. I am still not completely sure what he does but I am proud of him.

Goodness, I really am babbling now, but I'll press on – hope you're still reading!

My sister is two years younger and was, in turn, often deployed to assist my projects. If I saw Duncan as my enslaver, I of course saw myself as my little sister's empowerer as I sub-contracted my chores to an ever-obliging Soph. She was also only allowed to be the assistant to my 'vet' in the animal practice I established in our cubbyhouse. I was the classic middle child, perhaps, manipulated by the older and manipulating the younger.

And I of course got to choose which ABBA girl I was (always Frida) as we sung into our hairbrushes, blind cords and at least once, our pet budgerigars, who we would 'liberate' in our bedroom despite Dad being highly bird-phobic. Sophie liked Sherbet, I like Skyhooks and she was, still is, a horsey girl while I love my animals to be smaller than me. She lives with her family on the Peninsula so we don't see each other that often, which is a pity.

Robin, does that give you an idea?

Best

Susannah

I read it through. I seem to have shared rather a lot rather quickly but it feels okay. I email it through to Maddy and go back to bed and, finally, sleep.

Susannah, 3 September

It is Emma's fifteenth birthday. Family tradition dictates that she is woken by family carrying a tray bearing a lit candle, a Swedish flag and her presents. She is also subjected to the less than harmonious voices of her family singing 'Happy Birthday'. Although tradition also dictates that the birthday person be asleep and woken to this lovely family gesture they never are – the excitement of the presents being too much – but Emma dutifully goes through the motions of pretending to rouse on our entry. I love my kids' birthdays: I love seeing their faces as they unwrap their presents, as they read my annual 'Mum letter' (which, apparently, is too emotional) and I love the hug I give and get.

It is with a happy heart that I drive the kids to school after Emma's birthday ritual and then return to my desk – and an email from Maddy.

Email from Maddy to Susannah, 9.10am

Good morning Susannah,

I really enjoyed reading your letter, and your sense of humour. Thanks for letting me take a peep at it. I feel you have offered more in the letter, but the tone and pace continues to be measured. I think that's what you want.

I'll wait for your green light before I send this letter off.

Email from Susannah to Maddy, 9.17 am

Morning Maddy

Thanks again and glad you think it's okay – I suppose you have to put yourself, your personality, out there a little if you want to progress a connection. Can feel a bit exposing but nothing ventured …

Please send it off.

'If you want to progress a connection.' Where did that come from? Is that me saying that? Is that what I want to do? I didn't think that until I wrote it, but maybe it is. What happened to just finishing things up better?

And now Maddy, working part-time, is not back in the office until Wednesday. Why am I so edgy about having to wait?

Increasingly I am getting the feeling that I am not in control of what's happening.

Robin, 4 September

What a generous, warm and amusing letter! She's so easy to connect with. I love her wry sense of humour. But the second paragraph – it's very apologetic. Full of fear of offending, of being disapproved of, for doing, saying – being – wrong. (It's not hard to understand why – poor little thing!)

What will I say about bedside books? I know what would be safe and 'in tune', but I have to tell the truth. I know the Bible is not exactly going to help her feel connected to me, and that a born-again Christian is often regarded as a bit of weirdo, but I have to declare my colours from the beginning; it just gets harder later. I am not planning to be a closet Christian, so I have to show who I am, for better or worse. It's no good her getting to know a false me.

I have to say, though, when Susannah says she's a baby, baby Buddhist I feel that old, familiar twinge of fear regarding my children: Oh, no! They must know Jesus. What if they don't? I'm fully aware this is my insecurity – a weak place in my trust in God, and very counterproductive to His workings. Lighten up, Robin! Perhaps go with 'Cheers', instead of 'Love' for a change.

Discombobulated

Susannah, Monday, 8 September

No email from Robin in the morning. Nor in the afternoon. Finally I ring FIND: Maddy is not in the office today. There won't be an email.

My heart, inexplicably, sinks and I feel really disappointed.

Susannah, Tuesday, 9 September

I ring FIND at 9am; if there's a problem I want to be on it early. Maddy is not in today either and I wonder if she is okay (I ask, they don't divulge; policy I guess) but then I feel panicked, weirdly deprived and a little desperate. I channel my energy into stalking the FIND office – there must be someone I can speak to. And, finally, it seems there is: I speak to Maddy's manager and ask if she can access Maddy's email.

But what is this, what am I doing? Why do I care so much? I don't know but I calm down when an email arrives forwarding a letter – and photo – from Robin that she had written on the weekend. Something in me quietens when I realise she had actually responded quickly.

Email from Robin to Susannah, 11.40am

Hi Susannah,

I am writing this believing by faith that my daughter, Marian, will be able to attach the two photos I got her to take of me yesterday. I did choose the ones I considered flattering so the reality of wrinkles, sagging neck, bad teeth, etc. has been minimised (vanity dies hard!). Also, I look like a blonde because I am transitioning to my natural grey, but I was a brunette originally.

Something else I need to clear up about my book: Marian says all she could find online was the last chapter 'Metamorphosis'. Is that all you read or did you somehow access the whole thing? If you didn't, I would rather you read it all. I could send you a copy. Even if you have read it all, I would be happy to give you one – personally signed of course! Perhaps it will show you what you may have been spared by your adoption – I mean all the chaos and turmoil.

In regards to other reading, I have to admit I am not at all au fait with new writers. Much of my reading does tend to be Christianity-related and I guess my main bedside book is the Bible. However, I love a good novel – but hard to find. I must read *Cold Comfort Farm*. I loved the 'classics': Dickens, Jane Austen, etc. – especially George Eliot; *Daniel Deronda* is a favourite. I also really like the poems of Gerard Manley Hopkins. As you see, very much past writers! On a light side I have enjoyed Clive James. Recently, first via op shop and then library, I discovered books by Rosamunde Pilcher (*The Shell Seekers* and *Coming Home*) which I really enjoyed; they suited me in a comfortable way. I'm sure there are many great novels out there – I just don't know which they are.

Thanks for all the info on your siblings – very interesting and amusingly conveyed!

Cheers for now,
Robin

I stare at the photo. She's real, she exists now. She's no longer a concept, and this is what she looks like. Does she look like me? Do I look like her? I don't think so. Does she look nice? Yes. I think so, nice smile. What do I think about this? I have absolutely no idea.

I read her letter. And then I read it again. What do I make of it? She's a brunette and a Christian, and hard-core Christian it would seem. It's pretty much all she reads. Not sure which one – the hair colour or the Christianity – is more discombobulating. Neither is anything I can relate to. Or want to? And what does she mean I was 'spared'? Is she happy for that? Don't we all have bad stuff happen to us? Was hers a lot worse than others? And 'Cheers for now'? What's that about? She's gone all casual – why? Losing interest maybe? Already? Have I said something that jarred with her? My poor, over-thinking mind begins to race again and my heart is pounding. Do I reply? Where does this go next?

I'm not sure but I do feel I need to clear up about the book, so I shoot back a short email:

Email from Susannah to Robin, 11.53pm

Hi Robin

Many thanks for the photo; it helps make the hitherto conceptual real, if also a little bit discombobulating. Not sure why, I may just discombobulate easily, hence it being my favourite word . . .

However, a quick reply to answer your question about your book – I did read the whole book. Copies of all books published are lodged with both the State and National Libraries so, feeling slightly stealthy, I read it at the State Library.

I think everyone's lives have their serve of chaos and turmoil, don't you?

All best
Susannah

'Hitherto conceptual real.' When was the last time I said 'hitherto'? Have I ever said 'hitherto'? Anyway, it's a little too try-hardily expressed, but it's true – she wasn't real before, but now she is. And at least I've confessed/revealed/just mentioned I was discombobulated – I have to be honest, don't I?

Robin, 10 September

Hmm … what's gone wrong? I don't like this short note – it's terse and formal. Practical, efficient, but very cool.

What has offended her? What did I say wrong in my last letter? She does say she was discombobulated by it.

That last line: 'I think everyone's lives have their serve of chaos and turmoil, don't you?' actually sounds hostile. Or am I reading things into it?

Rereading my letter, looking for clues, all I can think of is that maybe I sound too flippant and too removed from her. I mention my daughter Marian twice in the space of two paragraphs; is that insensitive, like, 'This is my real family'? Then my comment about the chaos and turmoil – better you weren't there – now does strike me as glib and potentially hurtful, shutting her out.

Oh no! Throw in the photo of me and the Bible and she'd be feeling less and less like she has any part in my world.

I am convinced now that this is the problem: I gave the impression that I didn't really care and this was perhaps seemingly confirmed by my ill-timed decision to change my sign-off from 'love' to 'cheers'.

Oh dear, you have to be so careful. How can I fix this, or make it better?

I sit down to write back to Susannah, but I find it really hard. I am trying to make up for what I fear she has perceived as a cold and uncaring tone in my last letter, but it's not coming out right. I draft a reply and decide to run it past my sister, Susan, before I send it. I ring her and ask for her thoughts. What does she get from Susannah's short note? Am I being paranoid?

Susan tends to think I'm not and that I do have to reassure Susannah; but my draft is a bit weird – sort of suddenly 'over the top'. I don't want to appear unhinged!

So, I modify and moderate, and hope this version is all right. Email communication can certainly be tricky.

One thing is for sure: I'll abandon 'cheers' and go back to 'love'.

Susannah, 11 September

Email from Robin to Susannah, 4.22pm

Hi again Susannah,

I know what you mean by the fact of actually seeing a photo being discombobulating; I felt the same when I saw photos of you. I stared at them trying to compute the quite massive fact that this elegant, competent, mature woman was my daughter!

You used the phrase 'significant strangers'. This is true but for me the stranger factor is no match for the weight of the significance – and anyway, just from our short history of email exchanges, I already feel an ease of connection and that we are 'on the same wavelength'. (Hopefully you do too!) Then there's the deeper level of the heart significance, which is very real for me. I am very grateful that we are in contact. I do find it exciting I have to admit!

Remember, feel free to ask any question that you want.

Love, Robin

I jump on Robin's letter the moment the email arrives. I read it. I read it again. And, then, quite simply, I go mental. Something in me goes off the rails. My heart jumps up and hits me over the head. And I have no idea why.

Losing it

Susannah

I read Robin's letter over and over again, trying to work out what she has said that has me so spun out – and why I care.

'My daughter', 'ease of connection', 'same wavelength', 'heart significance'. Is that it? She is making connections. And then what's with the 'Remember'? Is she telling me what to do? I thought I was leading this operation!

But I'm not: it's a thing now and I realise it's gone beyond the writing-the-good-letter plan in which I apologise in a more empathetic way, and she says thanks and that's it. It's gone well beyond that. It was supposed to make us both feel good, resolved, settled, but now I am anything but.

What have I done? This was not a good idea. I don't want to feel this, whatever this is. I want to run away.

And so that's exactly what I do. I close the email and go back to my life. My real life – not whatever this is.

I run, I run a lot, playing ABBA songs through my headphones (a big tip-off that I am not okay) and I take the dogs for long walks on the beach. And, sometimes, I try to work out why I feel so utterly at sea. Most times, though, I just keep going: I pack the kids off to school, manage family life and work, write books, go to meetings, do my emails and keep up with friends. Yet all the time I feel that something is gathering, a bit like when you see the lightning and you're waiting for the thunder. And I don't want it to come, I don't want to feel it.

It's like I've opened a box, a Pandora's box that has not only spewed all its contents on the ground but has shaken up all the other boxes on the shelf as well – there is stuff everywhere.

The easiest thing would be to walk away, to close the box and pretend it never happened. And so that's what I try to do.

But I can't. I can't sleep, I find it hard to concentrate – I am a nearly fifty-year-old woman who was hitherto (hold on, there's that word again) highly competent and happy and now I seem to be losing it. And I can't work out why. I feel like I am wrestling all this stuff and the biggest thing I am wrestling with is Mum.

Mum. My wonderful, much-loved, much-missed mum. How can I be Robin's daughter if I am Mum's daughter? Does a 'connection', being on the 'same wavelength' with Robin, diminish my connection, my lifelong, heartfelt, time-tested connection with Mum? Can I take that risk?

Déjà vu

Susannah, 17 September

I know I have to send Robin a reply. I can't keep ignoring it, her. I think I know how to reply. I write the letter.

Email via FIND from Susannah to Robin

Hi Robin

I'm sorry I have taken a while to reply. I had a work deadline but also, I need to confess, I was a little 'spooked' by your last email.

The hardest thing for me to say and perhaps for you to hear is the same thing I think I said last time we had contact: I'm not sure where to put you in my life, where you fit in.

While I understand you see me as your daughter, I can't see you as my mother. I had, still have in my heart, a mother whom I, quite simply, adored and I can't let anyone else into that mother box, even bizarrely, I know, my biological birth mother. I don't want to disappoint you but I just can't do that. I, we, need to work out what I can do.

Déjà vu

To be really frank I think I have spent a lot of my life trying
to prove I was good enough, good enough to be kept, that I
deserved my seat at whatever table I was sitting or wanted
to sit at. I think part of that came from being given up, part of
it comes from Mum's early struggles as she grieved her lost
daughters at the same time as she tried to bond with her new
one, and part of it is just me. Mum and I discussed this a lot
(she did a lot of that, discussing, digging in for the truth) and
we both came to see that it's not about blame or fault, it's just
about what was, that everyone did their best. Everyone wonders
if they're good enough, I suspect, and I was no different, just
with the little kicker of a slightly confused start. And that led,
I think, to a lot of my striving for success – at school, at university
and in my various careers – to prove that I was good enough.

Ideally we balance yin and yang yet I have spent a lot of my
life yanging myself along, ever-questing. A lot of success and
wonderful opportunities have come from that but it's also a
little exhausting. This realisation finally came about when,
one after another, both my children became seriously ill and
I put myself in such full-throttle yang to help them I nearly
broke. Just before I did, I was lucky enough to be able to go
away for a week where I was nurtured as I recalibrated and
balanced my head and my heart.

The decision to contact you came from that time away.
I finally resolved that 'good enough' issue. I was good
enough, Mum was good enough and you were good enough.
We all were, are, and, as I said in my first letter to you this
time, I wanted to make sure you knew that. I've done that but
now I confess I don't know where to go next.

I don't know where that leaves us, perhaps finding a middle
way with some different words around it, words that don't

scare me or make me feel disloyal to Mum. The start is probably friendship.

How do you feel about all of that? I don't want to simply flip the situation around to me but find a way we are both happy to continue with.

All best,
Susannah

I send it to Maddy even though I know she now won't be in the office until Monday. I think it's done the job but I am still uneasy. Something is niggling at me and I feel unsettled.

Love Child?

Susannah

Driving back from a meeting I hear a piece of classical music, *I Giorni* by Ludovico Einaudi and I start to cry. I am the least musical person in my family – I was told to lip-sync in a Year 5 choir and my children still mock my exuberant but apparently talent-free singing – but I love listening to music and admire the way it makes me feel things. This piece cuts through me. It's beautiful, but why the tears? Really, Susannah, what's going on with you?

Luckily my family have all scattered for the weekend and I have some time alone, to see if I can sort myself out.

I come home, download the music, pour a glass of wine and play it loud. It really is beautiful, with a tentative fragility as the violin and the piano dance together – one edging forward then receding, then forward again, reaching out and responding, yearning and comforting. In my head the piano is Robin, lower, slower, steady, and the violin a more skittish me. I play it on a high rotation my teenage daughter Emma would envy and I sit and think.

As luck (or something) would have it, a mini-series about adoption is on TV at the time. *Love Child* follows a group of young women who enjoy the sexual freedom of the 1960s but without the benefit of the contraception of the next decade. It follows them as they enter a wing of a women's hospital in Sydney where they will each wait out their confinement before relinquishing their baby to a more 'suitable' married couple unable to have children.

So, I binge-watch it. I want to understand what happened back in 1965 in a way I have never wanted to before. I watch the whole series and, bit by bit, something in me crumbles. When I get to the scene where the baby is born, lifted out from behind a sheet so the mother can't see it, I can barely see through my tears. My mind can't help but flash between what I'm watching, the birth of my own two children, and wondering what my own birth must have been like – for both Robin and for me.

I realise I really haven't thought about this before. But now that I have, I'm thinking, feeling, that it must have been horrible – horrible for Robin and, for the first time, consciously anyway, horrible for me, the baby. A baby who must have been expecting to meet her mother.

And now I'm hooked and I want to understand more, every-thing, about adoption at the time. I hunt down and watch ABC documentaries from the 1960s proclaiming the wonderful work adoption was doing for single mothers and childless couples alike, and watch footage of babies crying, screaming in their horrible, hard hospital cribs. No one hugs them, no one loves them – they are alone. I Google adoption websites and read testimonials from birth mothers and children: they all talk of loss and grief.

Loss and grief. I have never thought about it in these terms before. Did I, do I, have that? How could that be? I had the most loving, wonderful family and, particularly, a mum and dad who loved me and whom I adored. How could I have loss and grief? What did I lose? What am I grieving?

But I keep reading and the words keep on appearing: separation, trauma, primal wounds, loss, genetic roots, genetic identity.

And, all of a sudden, this adoption thing isn't intellectual anymore – it's felt. It's something inside me. And it opens.

Still, indulgently now, playing *I Giorni*, I go to my desktop and Photoshop the photo of Robin with photos of me as a toddler, as a girl, and as I am now. I'm trying to visualise a connection to my beginning, to the place I started.

And I cry. A lot. I sit in it. That's what my baby Buddhist mindful training would have me do – sit in the feeling, not run away from it but feel it, explore it, watch it. I am fairly sure it doesn't say wash all that watching down with a few glasses of wine but I do that as well, desperate to pull the volume down a bit.

And I need to, because something big has been let out, with a ferocity that has scared me, and I don't know where to put it.

I really wish I could talk to Mum about it, so I kind of do. I imagine her saying, 'So, what's all this about, then?' in the way she would when I had clearly worked myself into a state. 'What's going on over there?'

'Well, there's this woman, Mum,' I reply. 'My birth mother, actually, and we've made contact and it's made me feel all weird.'

'Tell me about that, darling …'

And so I let Mum's patient, kind wisdom tease the emotion out of me, not letting me get away with histrionics and helping me work out what to do.

And I realise something, which I write in my journal:

It's okay, you can love two mothers. You have permission.

Whose permission? Mum's? I think so. No, I know so. She's okay with this.

So, l re-read the letter I've emailed to Maddy and realise I've pretty much written the same letter I wrote in 1989, the same letter I was supposed to be improving on – *Sorry, but I don't know what to do with you, still a bit tricky, hope that's okay, cheers.* I've written a letter that closes doors.

And, I realise, I do want to build a relationship with Robin after all, with my other mother.

So, urgently, I email Maddy again and ask her not to send the first letter. I tell her I need to write another letter, one that opens rather than closes.

Where has Susannah gone?

Robin

I'm getting a bit anxious now. This is definitely too long a gap since I've heard from Susannah. Still, I won't panic; she has other things going on in her life. I share my misgivings with Susan, who, unfortunately, can see my point. The silence is uncharacteristic.

But it's not possible, is it? This whole thing can't just vanish in a puff of smoke? The thought that maybe it could now grips my heart in fear. I couldn't take it; it would be too cruel a disappointment. The whole restored-daughter miracle, a fizzer? No, I actually do have more faith in God than that.

I go about my life, apparently as normal but not really. That awful anxious suspense within, invisibly tainting the everyday pleasures and pursuits of the present. Like when you are awaiting a doctor's report, the results of tests, about which they seemed to have some concern.

I hate living that underwater half-life. Time to do something useful: ring Maddy.

The call is both confirming and comforting. Yes, Susannah is going through something of an emotional crisis, but Maddy believes we will weather the storm. Will Maddy communicate my distress to Susannah? Am I allowed to ask if she will? I don't know. I'm not completely sure how she works. It may be better for me not to say anything.

Then, at last – re-emergence! Maddy calls to tell me she has a letter from Susannah to forward to me. It feels like I have surfaced from the bottom of the ocean and can breathe again.

Rewriting my feelings

Susannah, Sunday, 21 September

It takes me hours to rewrite the letter. I scrutinise every line, every word trying to ensure it says what I think I want to say, what I feel.

Hi Robin

Okay, just tweak the first line a bit maybe.

I'm sorry I have taken a while to reply. I had a work deadline but also, I need to confess, I was a little 'spooked' by your last mail **and needed to work out why.**

Then the first two paragraphs have to go; they're just a slightly wordier version of 1989's polite rejection. Is that what I want to do? I don't think so but I don't know what to say – well, say that then.

~~The hardest thing for me to say and perhaps for you to hear is the same thing I think I said last time we had contact: I'm not sure where to put you in my life, where you fit in.~~

~~While I understand you see me as your daughter, I can't see you as my mother. I had, still have in my heart, a mother~~

~~who I, quite simply, adored and I can't let anyone else into~~
~~that mother box, even bizarrely, I know, my biological birth~~
~~mother. I don't want to disappoint you but I just can't do that.~~
~~I, we, need to work out what I can do~~

To be completely honest, I am finding this all much more difficult and confusing than I ever expected to. I swing between being curious, and yes, excited, to being scared and wanting to run away so I don't hurt or disappoint anyone.

The next two paragraphs are fine, I think. I'm being honest, explaining how I got here, how I got to her. A little softening tweak, but I'll keep them.

I think I have spent a lot of my life trying not to disappoint, to prove I was good enough, good enough to be kept, good enough to deserve my seat at whatever table I was sitting or wanted to sit at. I think part of that came from being given up, part of it came from Mum's early struggles as she grieved for her lost daughters at the same time as she tried to bond with her new one and part of it is just me. Mum and I discussed this a lot in different ways at different ages (she did a lot of that, discussing, digging in for the truth) and we both came to see that it's not about blame or fault, it's just about what was, that everyone did their best. Everyone wonders if they're good enough, I suspect, and I was no different just with the little kicker of a confused start. And that led, I think, to a lot of my striving for success – at school, at university and in my various careers – to prove that I was good enough.

So, while we're supposed to balance our yin and yang, I have spent a lot of my life 'yanging' myself along, ever questing, to achieve, to be good enough. A lot of success and wonderful opportunities have come from that but it's also a little exhausting. This realisation finally came about when, one after another, both my children became seriously ill and I put myself in such full-throttle yang to help them I nearly broke. And then, just before I did break, I went away for a week – to be nurtured, to try to recalibrate my head and my heart – **and to stop thinking all the time so I could feel a bit more.**

Oh no! The next paragraph. Aaaaaaaarrrgggghhhh! That's pretty much the 1989 version too – we're all great, we're all forgiven. Game over. Not what you're trying to say, Susannah. You're not being honest about how you feel, you need to show how torn you felt when Robin called you her daughter: disloyal yet deprived at the same time. Try again.

The decision to contact you came from that time away.
I finally resolved that 'good enough' issue. I was good
enough, Mum was good enough and you were good enough.
We all were, are, and, as I said in my first letter to you this
time, I wanted to make sure you knew that. ~~I've done that but
now I confess I don't know where to go next.~~ **I did that but
I wasn't prepared for the maelstrom of feelings that have
followed since. As you can see, I haven't mastered this
thinking–feeling thing!**

The next bit is rubbish too. Does a friend make you feel this way? Come on, put it out there, you don't have to have all the answers.

~~I don't where that leaves us, perhaps finding a middle way
with some different words around it, words that don't scare
me or make me feel disloyal to Mum. The start is probably
friendship.~~

**I understand you see me as your daughter and I,
undeniably, feel something too; the significance is there,
I feel it dancing in my stomach as I write, but I can't quite**

wrangle it. I have been finding it really difficult to see you as my mother without feeling guilty and disloyal to Mum. I had, still have in my heart, a mother whom I, quite simply, adored and miss terribly, **and I don't know yet how to let someone else into that mother box, even bizarrely, I know, my birth mother. I don't want to disappoint or hurt you and I do want to know you and to meet you but I'm struggling with how it all fits together.**

Better. Now tell her you have spent a lot of time thinking about your birth – how it must have been for her, for you. Ask her how it was.

Maddy talks about the triangle of relationships and I've found that a helpful way to look at things and to re-look at things, to re-shape that box. And so, I've spent the last days trying to better understand your 'angle': I've wandered all over the Internet, watched the Jan Russ *Australian Story* and the 1965 *Unmarried Mother* documentary and I've re-read the rather sparse folder of my birth records. I started off trying to think through it all and ended up trying to feel it, to feel the story, yours and mine, behind all that cold paperwork.

But you're here, so perhaps, if it's okay, I could ask you to tell me the story of my birth again. You have asked if I have questions and I've been dodging that because the ones I have are the really big ones and I'm not sure why I can't remember everything you wrote in your first letter: what happened at my birth; what happened immediately after; how you felt? They're really big, huge, and they block any smaller, easier ones.

Okay, how to finish? Nup, that's not it, too cold. Try again.

~~How do you feel about all of that? I don't want to simply flip the situation around to me but find a way we are both happy to continue with.~~

Robin, I hope this all makes some kind of sense to you and doesn't spook you back. Most of all, I hope I don't hurt you. I'm not blocking, I'm just needing to move carefully, trying to find a path that doesn't scare me or make me feel disloyal to Mum, but also recognises you, me, us.

And then sometimes I think I should just stop thinking and go with the feeling,

Nice, I think. And then I stop and think and make one more change – a change that changes everything

~~All best~~
love,
Susannah

There I said it, love. Do I love her? I think I probably do. But how does that work? In what way? How can you possibly love someone you have never met? How can you love someone you don't know? You can't, can you?

So, what is it that is drawing me towards Robin?

Something opens

Susannah, Monday, 22 September

Email from Maddy to Susannah

Hi Susannah,

I just got off the phone to Robin who said she managed to read your email. She wanted you to know she thought it was beautiful and she loved your openness. She asked me to pass on she loved it so much she wants to take the time to give it the response it deserves.

I hope you can rest easy while you wait for a reply knowing how much it meant for Robin to receive that letter.

Feel free to be in touch tomorrow, Susannah.

Be kind to yourself,
Maddy

Robin, Tuesday, 23 September

So, it was my last letter that spooked her. I thought it was the one before, and the last one was my attempt to correct that. But I never did feel that letter was quite right, despite several drafts. Anyway, clearly something had gone wrong, but thank God she's back!

So sad, her feeling she always has to perform for approval. And that awful, irrational guilt – that somehow she's a Jonah, a bringer of suffering and ill-fate, a curse, not a blessing. What a deception!

Then in the second-last paragraph, that huge question again: 'tell me about my birth ... tell me how you felt'. She admits she has been dodging it (as have I). Why? The unvoiced fear that just maybe she actually wasn't wanted, that I was not forced to give her up – that I chose to?

And my fear is: how will she judge me when she learns that that is the truth?

The letter Susannah has written is beautiful and brave. How I answer it will be crucial. Lord, help me to get it right!

This is what I write:

Email from Robin to Susannah, 11.10 am

Dear Susannah,

Thank you for your wonderfully open and honest letter –
I really appreciate it.

Firstly, I want to say that I totally understand your feelings of not wanting to betray your mother and not wanting her place to be usurped in any way. I would feel exactly the same in your place. As I seem to recall saying in my original letter, written so many years ago, a 'mother' is someone who raises, nurtures, cares for the child and goes through all the attendant joys and pains of such a role. I was not that for you and I would never presume to encroach on that relationship. I'm sorry if my last email gave that impression.

Our relationship is something else; it has its own unique reality and significance which we are both in the process of exploring.

Although I am not your mother in the all-important
'lived-out' sense, I think there are certain common, in-built
factors which hold true for any parent/child relationship.
For example, as children always are in this world of ours,
you were the totally innocent party in the whole un-ideal
situation, but you suffered from it anyway, and again, as is
so often the case with children, you assumed a 'guilt' and a
responsibility and an 'onus of proof' that never belonged to
you. Those feelings of 'I am not good enough', 'I am bound
to disappoint somewhere down the line' and the tension and
exhaustion of performance-based acceptance are so awful.
As you say, most people harbour some fear of inadequacy
(I certainly did), but to be given away at birth undoubtedly
would insert the rejection more efficiently. Your phrase
'good enough to be kept' is so sad. I'm so sorry for that,
Susannah!

As the adult parent, the responsibility for the situation was
all mine, not yours, and you have nothing to prove to me;
nor is it your responsibility to protect me from hurt and
disappointment.

However, I can assure you anyway that nothing you might do
or not do will disappoint me in the sense of thinking less of
you. I would be disappointed if our contact fizzled out, but I
would not be disappointed in YOU.

Just as the negative self-judgement that you were possibly
not good enough to be kept is clearly not based on reason
(as the little baby has done nothing either good or bad at
that point), but is a spiritual and emotional thing, so it is with
the bond of love I feel with you for the simple fact that you
are my child even though I have never seen you – even as a
baby. This bond places no expectations on you and is not

dependent on reciprocity. So you're stuck with that – hope you're not too spooked!

You asked for details of your birth, etc., and I want to tell you everything, but can we make it the next installment? That will also be a lengthy epistle and I think a breather is necessary!

Love, Robin

Susannah, Tuesday, 23 September

I cried as I read the letter. Something in me cracked open: it sounds corny but it's true, it's the only way I can describe it. I send Robin the link to *I Giorni* and I write this:

Email from Susannah to Robin, 12.29pm

Dear Robin

Thank you, thank you for your email – I was dreading having to wait. It made me cry in a completely good way.

Gustav Mahler said, 'If a composer could say what he had to say in words, he would not bother trying to say it in music.'

So I wanted to share this piece of music with you, I hope you can play the link – if you can't it's *I Giorni* by Einaudi with the violin by Daniel Hope. I came across it and it has now become inextricably tied to this unique experience of our contact.

It feels like a morning emerging, with a beautiful but tentative fragility as the violin and the piano dance together – edging forward then receding, then forward again, reaching out and responding, yearning and comforting. And it feels like coming home.

love,
Susannah

Susannah, 24 September

And then early, too early, the next morning I also write this:

Email from Susannah to Robin, 4.37am

Dear Robin

Thank you again for your letter. I can't tell you how much it meant. And I'm not spooked, quite the opposite.

The last couple of weeks have been this ever-swirling mixture of excitement and fear (discombobulated doesn't begin to describe it) but the strength and clarity of your letter released something in me and let things fall into a different, calmer, lighter place.

It helped me realise I don't need the boxes to put people in – a heart has infinite capacity if we let it and loving another person doesn't diminish the love for someone else.

I have two mothers that love me, and, as you say I'm stuck with that – or I'm blessed. I think I'll go with blessed.

So, at the risk of rushing, that seems a good place to meet from and take another step along this unique path. I would really like to and hope you do too.

love,
Susannah

Email from Maddy to Susannah and Robin, 11.00am

Dear Susannah and Robin,

As discussed here is a virtual exchange of your email addresses for you to start communicating directly.

Maddy

And then we were off ...

There was a little voice inside me saying *Careful, don't break this.* But I couldn't hear it above the roar.

IV

CLICK AND CONNECT

Click, click, click

Susannah, Wednesday, 24 September

Email from Robin, 1.38pm

Dear Susannah,

Words can't express how blessed I feel by the unfolding of
our relationship. It's sort of feels like a wonderful dream –
but actually I know it is the reality of redemption. I am so
grateful! Your last email before this one was completely
beautiful. I wanted to reply earlier but my deficient computer
can't play the music so I am waiting till I can hear it
tomorrow on another one. I am so glad my letter helped and
you are right – love is a strange commodity in that the more
we give (and receive) the more there is; no-one is made
poorer. Yes, you do have two mothers who love you and
we are both privileged to have you as our daughter
(I suspect your mother and I may have had a few things
in common!).

How can you ask whether I want to continue our walk of discovery?!! As for the risk of rushing, it strikes me that both of us are maybe a bit of the rushing ilk (to use a rather weird expression). I know I can err on the side of rashness versus slow caution. However, we are slowed in our tracks by the fact that I have my 6-year-old granddaughter staying with me and, although delightful, she virtually talks non-stop and gives me very little private space – especially not the headspace you need for something very important. It is something of a miracle that I am succeeding to write this email with relatively few interruptions. (My last long letter to you I wrote in the middle of the night.) I know I can't write the promised second installment till I have my peaceful solitude again – which will be next Tuesday. I do love you, Susannah,

Robin

Email from Susannah, 2.00pm

Dear Robin

Part of me is a bit jealous of that delightful six-year-old … so there you go, some evidence that you're right, I'm indeed a rusher not a caution person. I spend a lot of time wondering if I should try the caution thing some time. Not today obviously so I hope it's okay I reply so quickly. I have teenagers who spend their holidays flaunting their independence, so I have more space.

I don't mind waiting for the 'big' letter but might it be okay if we email a little in between, six year olds permitting? I don't want to spam you but I do want to keep 'talking' if that's okay?

Love,
Susannah

Email from Robin, 6.40pm

Dear Susannah,

'Delightful six year old' has been taken out for 1 hour, so here I am. Please don't think I am fitting you in around the edges. I long to concentrate on this enormous and wonderful turn of events – this newfound relationship with you. To be honest, I am hanging out for Tuesday! It is quite exhausting looking after such a young child for an extended period (remember my relative decrepitude!) – and harder when you have something else you want to be doing – i.e. focusing on you and me. Of course we can talk before Tuesday, but because it is all so huge emotionally, I want to give full attention to our communications – especially when I try to recount the events of 1965. Also, I would love to hear any more details about you and your life that you may care to share.

Love, Robin
ps. we are both speedsters, aren't we?! x

Email from Susannah, 6.53pm

Hello,

I understand, would you prefer to just wait until Tuesday? That's very mature of me to say that because I would really like to email a little before then but I can pull myself together if you think that's better.

Am mindful that I do belt out at things once I think it's safe and I don't want to break this by belting.

Let me know. Is there anything particular about me you want to know, it's a little hard to know where to start …

Love,
Susannah

Email from Robin, 7.03pm

Dear Susannah,

Don't you dare pull yourself together! I think it's rather hilarious how alike we are in this belting respect, and we are not going to break anything because neither of us want it to break. So fear not and TALLY HO!

Love, Robin

Email from Susannah, 7.09pm

Funny. Okay then, can you give me a steer on what you would like to know – and I can babble away while you mind granddaughter or recover from same. x

Email from Robin, 7.11pm

About your family?

Email from Susannah, 7.14pm

Too vague – more help please

Email from Robin, 7.21pm

But as I know so little, anything is good. You did tell me about your siblings; what about your husband? Emma and Edvard? With their permission of course. Do you have pets? Just babble as you feel like.

Email from Susannah, 7.26pm

Okay – have just cooked Emma's dinner in a very low-focus way but will attempt good mothering and then babble, if that's okay. I assume granddaughter (okay, what's delightful's name?)

will be back soon and need her grandmother, so just to manage my expectations do you think that will then be it for tonight? X

Email from Robin, 7.33pm

Great. Yes, Aziza will be back in full force soon. Maybe if she goes to bed not too late, I will get another email off tonight. If too tired, will definitely manage some reply to babble tomorrow. X

Email from Susannah, 7.39pm

Can't find a photo – really. One of my life goals is not to be in photos – it nearly killed me having to have the author pics you can see on the website.

Good luck with Aziza, what a good grandmother x

And then over three emails I babble on about my family …

Email from Susannah, 7.59pm

hello again

You still haven't been very helpful about where to start but here goes, with apologies in advance for babble (are you sure I can't break this?).

Husband. Oskar. Incredibly good-looking Swede. Our marriage is, we joke, a one-night stand that just got out of control but 22 years later we're still together.

He is annoying because he doesn't seem to age while I do – I suspect it's those Nordic genes but it feels like we are living *The Portrait of Dorian Gray*.

So anyway, we met at a Christmas party. Emma hates this

94

story because it shows the fragility of fate and the 'what if?'.
Oskar had arrived in Australia, backpacking, a month before
and met up with two other Swedes, one of who (whom?)
knew a family in Melbourne. They bought an old car and
meandered down the east coast ending up with said family
and said family's mother instructing older son to take Swedes
to Christmas party – which he grumpily did.

Cut to Christmas party.

I have a friend, Sally, who was, is, excellent at loving life and
she announces – 'I have discovered there are three Swedes at
this party and I think we should each have one for Christmas!'
(You have to tell if I offend you.) She tells me which one she
has selected and I look at the others and, I promise, I still
remember looking at Oskar and thinking, that one, definitely.

Anyway, I spend a lot of time trying to be interesting and
interested and, hurrah, he has a girlfriend, coming to meet
him in Byron Bay. How excellent! So I stop being interested
and probably interesting and wish him well.

But then he keeps appearing at Christmas parties (we are
23, just out of uni and I am back living at home because I am
broke) and then, badly (of him, not me, I was single) we share
a moment, an extended moment.

I am definitely thinking it's a one-night stand (too much to tell
you? – please let me know) but what a lovely boy and I really
must go to Sweden when two weeks later I get a call – can he
come back to Melbourne?

Well, yes he could and he did. We spent three completely
unrealistic months together and then he returned to Sweden.
Ten months later I got on a plane to bring him back here.
On paper, a ridiculous decision but we're still here.

Okay, that's a sampler. I need some guidance here if you are up for this. Mum used to talk, mostly affectionately, about my 'oppressively high spirits' and I don't want to inflict them on you or completely disobey the wonderful Maddy who has counselled to go slow.

x

Email from Susannah, 9.02pm

Okay, last babble mail – I really am slightly scared I will over-belt and break this.

Do you want to see any photos of when I was younger? As part of me trying to work through stuff when I received your photo (thank you – not sure I said that because I was too busy being spooked) I made up a composite of your photo, my photo now, and two when I was a child. Maybe it seems strange but it actually comforted rather than confronted – but that's me, it may not be for you.

Robin, I'm really aware I have just belted away tonight and I hope that really is okay. I have to say it's felt very natural and I am lucky enough to be able to bat my family off so I can focus on this – six year olds are not so easy but, once again putting my heart out there, perhaps just let me know it's been okay, or not. X

Email from Susannah, 10.46pm

Make that second-last babble – and not withstanding my fear that I have over-babbled …

As I was waiting up to see if you might reply tonight (my problem, not yours, sorry) I wondered if you understood when I said we seemed in a good place to meet I meant physically meet? For me, it seems the next step in making things concrete and part of real life. I confess I find thinking about it (which I have a lot these last days) both exciting and scary but much more exciting than scary and I am much more scared of it not happening than it happening.

What do you think?

Robin, I assure you, I am not this needy normally but this is, as you say, so emotionally huge so I am pretty stripped bare and vulnerable, trying to balance safe with honest but ending up just stripped back.

I hope you slept well, ready for a lovely day with Aziza x

Susannah, Thursday, 25 September

Email from Robin, 1.27am

Hello – here I am at 12.50am, courtesy of a toilet visit. Aziza came back bearing Roses chocolates and we watched *Singin' in the Rain* for the second time today. I ate six chocolates straight off, 'rewarded' by horrific sight in mirror later. (I have been too slack with my diet lately – too much temptation with things bought for kids in the house, and I am already definitely fatter than in those photos I sent you.) I fell into bed at about 9.45 and was almost instantly asleep.

Susannah, you haven't over-babbled at all – I was expecting lengthier, stream of consciousness type ravings I think!

Thank you so much for the photo of your children; they really are beautiful! Yes, we will have quite a lot of more serious things to share further down the track probably. Would you consider sending me that composite photo you made?

Actually, I didn't realise you meant physically meet in that letter. Of course I want to (also a bit scared); my vision for the future is so full-on and comprehensive that I wouldn't dare divulge it for fear of spooking you completely!

love, Robin x

I get up early, before I need to hustle the kids to school, and check my emails like a child checking their Christmas stocking. I am disproportionately happy to see a new message in my inbox. I read it and am at once reassured and excited. I send a reply and attach the photo composite I made when I was going mental.

Email from Susannah, 5.02am

Hello

Up for same reason although I confess this experience has not been brilliant for my sleeping, too much adrenalin I think.

Here is the photo composite. You obviously, me about two years ago when having to have photos taken, me around the age of ten, and me around two. They were not selected for their ages, nor any other reason, they are just the ones I have on my computer (although we would have to be very close indeed before I released any photos from the 80s – what were we all doing?).

I hope it's okay for you seeing the photos. As I said, it was quite a moment for me (and there have been a few this last week) but it was a comforting one, one of inevitability, of necessity even.

Please don't think me rude that I'm not asking about your family, I need a little time to get my head around that and, frankly, I am happy for it just to be about you, us, for now. Is that okay?

Back to bed for I hope a little more sleep now. *Singin' in the Rain* can probably bear high rotation – my go-to films are, to my kids' horror, unspeakably daggy, apparently – *Sound of Music* and *Mamma Mia* (of course). x

Email from Susannah, 7.37am

Morning spamming now, sorry but just checking all okay after photo ... X

Email from Robin, 7.37am

Frustration! My technical incompetence has struck! I opened your email with photos but it didn't all fit on page. Pressing buttons wildly (predictably) didn't help. That 'box' icon wasn't there. So, I can't read it all – nor see all the photos.

Email from Robin, 8.21am

Thank you! Have seen photos, but not all words of that email yet. Love Oskar email. Really want to reply properly, Susannah, but I have to go about my commitments today now. You must know there is nothing I would rather do than stay chatting on computer, but apart from other duties, Aziza is the perfect example of your mother's phrase 'oppressively high spirits!'

So, an enforced break. But I love, and am completely enjoying, our correspondence.

love, Robin x

Email from Robin, 9.39pm

Hi! Aziza asleep, so I can return and re-read your recent emails. Looking at the composite photos: three things. Firstly, the one of me may as well be photo shopped – I look older in real life; the one of you is good but of course it's the one I have already seen on the Net (do you have more and any of you in your 20s? Or is that the dreaded 80s I suppose?); thirdly, the ones of you when you are little are adorable – what a dear little face! They do stir up feelings of sadness and yearning in me for what might have been. But a different path was taken and I am trusting, as ever, in the power and willingness of Jesus to redeem our messes and even make something beautiful out of them. I certainly am aware of the great beauty in this reconnection of ours – it has surpassed my hopes. You are just such a warm and alive person (and so clever and funny as a bonus!). What did I do to deserve such a gift? Nothing of course, but I am thrilled with it, with you.

I like daggy films too – including those two you mention. Do you have any other favourites you can think of?

I will close now and send this in hope that you can read it tonight. Lots of love x

Email from Susannah, 9.47pm

Hello, that was nice – thought I'd just check one more time and there you were.

Did you manage to play the music today?

Email from Susannah, 9.50pm

Here's a picture of me around 1989 …

Email from Robin, 9.58pm

O my goodness, how gorgeous! Big family likeness I have to say.

The emails ping back and forth slightly feverishly and we begin to talk about meeting.

Email from Robin, 10.29pm

When shall we meet, do you think? I feel a bit like we are reckless truants without Maddy's wise restraints.

Email from Susannah, 10.43pm

That's funny, I was thinking the same thing about Maddy – and we are both going to have to fess up on Monday.

She's completely right of course about taking time to process and not rushing but she seems to have two bolters on her hands.

I did talk to her about what a meeting might look like – I thought she might be a calming person to start with but I said I didn't want to meet in her offices – she's beautiful, they are ugly – and something special should take place somewhere special. Have been thinking about Botanical Gardens.

Bolter me says next week – too scary? X

Email from Robin, 10.46pm

Bolter me says sounds possible but let's sleep on it. Night. x

Spinning tops, slightly wobbly

Susannah, Friday, 26 September

Email from Susannah, 5.32am

I'm sorry it took me so long to be able to come to you Robin.

But I also know it could only have happened now, and been like this now. I think I needed all the things, good and bad (but mainly bad as I suspect they are our greatest teachers) to bring me here.

And I am so happy to be here X

But where is 'here' and how did I get here?

Email from Robin, 7.43am

Good morning! I agree. This is the right time, given all the factors, I am so happy, too.

Re our bolter idea of maybe meeting next week, a spirit of self-control has alighted and I think maybe the week after might be better as an option. If I am going to write that longer account of my pregnancy and your birth (those events I did not put in my book), then you will need time to process that. I think it is good if we deal with major questions before we meet. Do you agree? X

Email from Susannah, 7.47am

Morning. Hmmmm … is my attempt at a measured response to waiting another week.

Or you could say they might be better dealt with once we have – the meeting, though enormous, is only another step in a not necessarily linear walk.

Hello! The adult has returned, being mature, saying sensible things – thank goodness, I have been missing her. Then this.

Maddy will agree whole-heartedly – I agree whole-headedly, but not heartedly.

Good bye adult, hello needy child. That was brief, better get the adult back again …

Email from Susannah, 7.54am

I need to have a button that says 'Don't send for five minutes while you have a proper think' on my mail …

Sorry, Robin, that was selfish and maybe a bit six-year-old petulant. Of course.

Sorry
X

Email from Robin, 8.01am

Why don't we be guided by Maddy in this? We will both be talking to her Monday.

And now my dear wild horse, a further bridle – I have to go now and tonight I am sleeping over somewhere else so will not be able to chat. I will hear the music though, God willing. I will be home in time to watch Grand Final on telly.
Xx

Email from Susannah, 8.05am

Well, poop all around!

Suppose I'll have to do a lot of running (to burn off this energy) and some work. Then Maddy will absolutely say wait, so poop again.

Off bolting again, will miss you tonight but have a lovely time wherever you're going.
X

Email from Robin, 8.08am

xxx

I read over all the emails – why *did* I write that early-morning one? Am I sorry it took me so long to connect with Robin? Really? I have had the most wonderful life, loved and loving: I don't regret my wonderful family for a moment. Where is all this coming from and what's with the pushy and needy stuff? I seem to be in real danger of over-correcting – over-connecting? – here, from writing just one, resolving letter to stalking a woman I don't know. But yet I do seem to know her.

Mental. I need to slow down.

Robin

I'm feeling a little bit overwhelmed. Wonderful, but full-on. Like the tumbling surf has got too strong and I'm beginning to be dumped by the waves. I feel like I can't keep up with the pace and demands of the situation.

It's time for the loved and lovable puppy to stop jumping up on the old woman just now. She needs a rest, a break – not from her, but with her.

I need to catch my breath.

Susannah's inner child goes nuts

Susannah, Friday, 26 September

Robin has headed off to her life for the weekend and I don't know what to do with myself. Ridiculously, I feel abandoned.

Fifty-year-old me gets it completely: it's actually good to take a break on this fast-moving exchange for a while, take the time to get our breaths back. Maybe even spend some time with my poor, neglected husband. But the baby within me seems to have woken up with a hunger and ferocity and it's throwing all of its toys out of its cot – and the fifty-year-old sensible person right out the window.

I didn't really understand it then, but now I know we all have an inner child that can, if left untended, wreak havoc in our adult life when roused. My inner child had roared up and taken control. I knew something was up, wrong even, but I couldn't work it out – it was like trying to push the off button from inside the blender.

Feeling dizzy from the spinning and needing to find that off button, I take to my meditation cushion.

I became interested in meditation about three years ago. I was driven to find something that might offer some relief from the constant over-thinking and questioning that came with Mum's death and then the illnesses of my two children; I needed to put some space between me and my reeling thoughts and emotions. I try to practise Shamatha meditation – peaceful abiding – to train the mind in stability, clarity and strength. All three of these qualities seem to have deserted me at the moment.

You are supposed to simply sit and focus on the singular thing that is your breath. You watch it come in and out and, as thoughts swing in over the top, you acknowledge them as thoughts, as distractions, and then gently let them go, separate yourself from them and return to the certainty and unambiguity of your breath. Over time, one learns to tame the monkey-mind that jumps from one thought to another, incapable of keeping still, and moves to the calm equanimity that is something approaching a Buddha mind.

But you don't meditate to become good at meditating, you meditate to become better at life, so you can put the same stillness into your life and you can learn to respond rather than react when stuff happens. And when you can do that, you can become kinder and more compassionate – to yourself and to others.

That's the theory, anyway. I am very much still at the monkey-mind stage, but it has helped me at least to see, if not hold back, the mind-storms that have so often threatened to tip me over. And now, more than ever, I need some distance from these storms. But it's hopeless. As I sit on my cushion, thoughts of Robin and what I am doing crash through constantly and I have a whole jungle of birth-mother monkeys screeching at the tops of their monkey mouths. Completely hopeless.

So, I decide to channel my energies on the issue that appears to be obsessing me and I write Robin a long, long letter, babbling about my life, my work, my past, present and future. I know she's not on email to read it but it seems one way to hold on to our fragile connection.

You really haven't been very helpful in saying what you want to know about me so I have just taken a bit of a wander ...

What's important?

My family and friends. Obviously.

Laughing. Contrary to most of what you have seen of me so far, trying not to take anything, particularly me, too seriously.

I spent a lot of time at school being sent out of class for not being able to stop laughing (talking, too, actually – part of me really does want to be that quiet, wise woman in the corner who speaks rarely and softly but with great considered wisdom but it's not going to happen.) and have had to leave meetings to 'collect' myself. I need to get a grip – or actually do I?

All my close girlfriends are funny, they make me laugh a lot.

Oddly for someone with zero musical ability I also like singing, particularly daggy 80s songs, advertising jingles and inserting same, ideally both, into conversations – absolutely kills my kids, which in turn is also amusing.

ABBA. That is not a joke. They are really important. They are like chardonnay (which I also love) – much maligned but, as time will show, classy and enduring.

Favourite ABBA songs –

– Dancing Queen – unoriginal but who cares. I can and do listen to it 7 times in a row when I run along the beach in the morning. (Not that I'm a runner – used to hate the idea, haunted by the idea that if I ran some-where, I would then have to run back ... But I started slowly two months ago and I have to say that it has been really good for me, particularly with all the nervous energy that's been swirling around ...) Anyway, back to ABBA. When happy play 'Dancing Queen', when sad, play 'Dancing Queen'. Life is always better with 'Dancing Queen'.

- *Honey, Honey – weirdly, was as on high rotation when I was pregnant with Emma and once out she would always calm to it.)*
- *Dum Dum Diddle – possibly one of their more ridiculous songs but …*
- *Knowing Me, Knowing You – ahaaaaa …* Arrival *best album ever.*
- *Super Trouper – a late entry into my top 5, nudging out Mamma Mia.*

Animals – for most of my childhood I wanted to be a vet but I just wasn't good enough at science. (I also wanted to be a tennis player, a doctor, actor, journalist and then, just when it might have been really handy to know, in Form 6, I had no idea.)

We had five cats growing up – one came with the house, then each child had a cat and then I adopted a stray; two male budgies which turned out to be one girl and one boy and then we had three; mice (didn't last long due to five cats); terrapins (which Dad threw out because he thought they were dead but they were just sleeping really, really still); and the odd stray bird with a broken wing which Mum would let us keep.

We now have two dogs – Bella, a cavoodle, and Bill, a small Jack Russell. Bill is nearly 10 and losing his boyish energy but still very handsome in a George Clooney kind of way. Really. Bill is Edvard's spirit dog – unsure to start but if you're in, you're in, and good luck with getting out. Bill also thinks he is a German Shepherd.

Bella is Emma's spirit dog. She is happiness in a dog. She is an enthusiast who has a poor sense of boundaries and wants to make friends with everyone. Not everyone wants to make friends with Bella but this does not deter her. I sometimes wish it would.

X

Susannah, Saturday, 27 September

I open my emails and Robin has replied. I am ridiculously happy.

Email from Robin, 10.05am

Lovely to get your email. I am still not home, so this is just a short note and I will reply later tonight at greater length. I love it; it needs to be responded to properly when I am not distracted.

I have listened to the music, which is beautiful! Tender, tremulous, yet hopeful and capable of great things – like you.

Till later, love. X

She writes lovely things and, again, sensible, mature-woman me gets it. Inner-child nut job, however, is furious at the short email. It would seem no amount of kind words, compliments or attention is going to satisfy her.

Sensible me realises I have to try to wrangle all this feeling into some kind of thought, so I draft yet another email to Robin. I title it the 'serious email'.

Dear Robin,

Last Friday night I watched the last two episodes of *Love Child* (do you know it? It's a mini series about girls in Sydney in the 60s who give up their babies for adoption).

I watched an episode with one of the babies being born and a sheet going up in front of the mother just before she delivered and something broke – or maybe broke through – in me.

I think it is telling that I can't remember what you wrote last time about my birth. I wasn't forgetting but blocking, blocking something that perhaps I didn't want to know, to see – and on Friday I did.

110

Susannah's inner child goes nuts

For the first time, consciously anyway, I let myself be that little baby and feel really sad for it, for me. I was told that I screamed a lot in hospital – well, of course I did – I'd just been taken away from the person who had been my only sure reality.

So, it could have been a messy Friday night but it wasn't so bad because something had already been unblocked, released, by your beautiful letter last week.

And with that release came the really easy flow of communication we've been having which I have loved.

But the extent to which I have loved it has also worried me. This really strong, visceral feeling. I am so keen to have your every email and I jump on every compliment and affection. As I said, wanting approval, hunting for acceptance.

A little in parenthesis now. Robin, this is so totally weird, isn't it? I don't know you yet I am laying myself absolutely bare in front of you. I can't tell you how exposed I feel and how much I hope it's okay to do this. To say I was vulnerable would be a major understatement. To tell you I am a little scared of how you will react is also one.

But please don't misunderstand me, I don't wish any of this away nor deny it. I just want to understand it. I've spent most of my life saying, thinking, feeling I was complete, that I had this adoption thing covered but now, clearly, that's not true – the reconnection with you has brought something to the surface that must have been buried very, very deep. And while I am so happy it has surfaced, it's thrown me out to sea. Is it the same for you?

Have I totally spooked you now? If I have, I'm so sorry but I don't know any other way to work this than with complete honesty.

Robin, I'm going to need your help. I think I need to be re-connected with you physically, concretely, before I hear about the disconnection. Does that make sense? I think I'd rather hear it – or read it – having come back into the safe harbour rather than still be on the open seas.

But all of this is just about me and, obviously, this isn't just about me, it's about us. Us, past, present and most of all, I hope, future.

Much love,

Susannah

Right, that's putting it – and me – out there. I am about to send it to Robin when I stop and decide to send it to Maddy instead. Full points to Susannah the sensible: while the inner child sulks at not having the immediate gratification of sending it to Robin, I am relieved that at least there is some part of me that remains a clear-ish thinking adult.

But then, that evening, Robin doesn't email as she said she would. I have a total tantrum in my head – I rage and determine that I'm over this whole reunion thing, it was a mistake, we should call it quits now. I should have left sleeping dogs and birth mothers lie.

But I can't. I need to see if I can get her to respond.

Email from Susannah, Saturday, 27 September, 11.37pm

Hello again,

I am going to go to bed hoping your silence tonight was a result of a day enjoyed not something I've said.

X

Email exhaustion

Susannah

Email from Robin, Sunday, 28 September, 10.29am

Susannah, you naughty girl! Of course my silence was not a result of something you said! If I were concerned about anything, as if I'd just go silent! I'm sorry. I went to bed really early last night, exhausted, and have only just now got back to my computer.

You must remember that old people like me are not constantly connected as you younger generation are. I sort of GO TO THE COMPUTER, GO ON THE INTERNET (have you seen *IT Crowd*?) as a distinct event. Weird, I know, but true. And I never use the Internet on my phone – too small and laborious.

I am now going out for the day – my sister's birthday. Will reconnect later tonight.

I love you. Xxxxxxxxxxxxxxxx

Email from Susannah, 11.49am

No, I'm sorry. And I don't want to be a cyber stalker – or any other kind of stalker.

I need to pull myself together. I am a nearly-fifty-year-old, normally competent woman feeling like a lost child again, wanting approval, hunting for acceptance. It's doing my head in.

Am off to get a grip! Hope you have a lovely day with your sister X

Email from Robin, 12.57pm

It's understandable, but know that you have all my approval and acceptance – and love x

I like Robin's reply but I have already decided I'm not going to email her again today. Not so much for her sake but mine. I need to stop being so needy. I make it through the afternoon but then think it would be rude to not reply in some way to her nice email. But not too much, Susannah; one email, just a short one.

Email from Susannah, 8.00pm

Thank you Robin x

Robin

I'm beginning to feel out of my depth again, that my supply of emotional reassurance is not equal to the demand; it is being drained dry. Maybe it's just email burnout: this is not my accustomed mode of communication, especially at this rate. It reminds me of the one time I went on the treadmill at the gym – my legs went faster and faster out of my control till I was literally spun off the machine.

I think we just need to change the medium of our relationship – get off the cyber-ride and walk on solid land. Actually meet in person. Yes, I think we should do that, I'll suggest it.

Email from Robin, 10.09pm

Hello. You know I really want to meet soon. Waiting is beginning to feel wrong and a bit too intellectual. My fear is that when you read my story of that time you will think I didn't have a good enough reason for giving you up and so you will not be able to forgive me. So, I am scared I won't have your acceptance and approval – and you would have more justification than I for withholding it. I have none – and I don't want any anyway. It is a pure undeserved gift for me if you can offer me love now. Remember, as I have said in an earlier letter, it is I, not you, Susannah, who caused hurt.

Email from Susannah, 10.53pm

Hello, can't sleep, keep checking phone and then your email – I hope you read this tonight so you can sleep a little calmer.

My 'serious' email is on a similar track and I agree about the meeting – I need you out of my head and back in my life.

Robin, I'm scared too – this has opened up something that I think I must have buried very deep.

But I'm not going to judge your/our story and I am going to love you. I am also scared, so we can both be scared together and start rebuilding.

Love,
Susannah x

Email from Robin, 11.05pm

Thanks for reply! Yes, I believe we can do this. Maddy tomorrow and then let's see. Good night. Love. Xx

Email from Susannah, 11.10pm

Okay – poor Maddy!

I should've said one more thing – I would like to meet before I read or am told about my birth. I would like to have begun to reconnect physically before learning about the disconnect – let me know what you think about that – after I hope a good night's sleep for us both. X

Susannah

So much for the one short email rule! And 'I am going to love you' – where on earth did that come from? Why am I so confident? No idea but I do know now that I absolutely need to meet her.

Out of our heads

Susannah

My family is blessed to have a small farm, which doesn't actually farm anything, ninety minutes out of Melbourne. A house on a hill surrounded by bush, it's a place we go to get away, to relax, to heal. We have celebrated there, mourned and made merry: it's a special place. Oskar suggests we spend a few days there to see if it might help slow things – I suspect he means me – down a bit.

But it doesn't slow down the emails.

Email from Susannah, Monday 29 September, 6.18am

Morning,

Worst night's sleep ever – hope you fared better?

But reading this in a book about adoption reunion made me feel a little better: 'Approaching a reunion is like throwing your emotions into a blender at high speed. Elation, despair, panic, fear, all mix together, churning in the pit of your stomach.'

So other people have pulled this off.

X

Email from Robin, 8.26am

Good morning! I am happy to meet before you read about your birth – you know what is best for you. Do you want me to read your 'serious' email first? Maybe that would be good? If so, you could send it today – Aziza is going out for a short time.

As to place of meeting, my two needs would be peacefulness and privacy. I'm not sure the Botanical Gardens could guarantee those things – weather, lots of people around. They could be lovely for a subsequent visit? Would my house – or yours – be out of the question? (No one else home of course!)

Love, Robin x

Email from Susannah, 8.36am

Hello,

I know what's best for me? Are you nuts?!

Yes Botanical Gardens has its problems. Is it okay if I say no to either house? I think I need to get us sorted before bringing in the rest of our respective lives – does that make sense? It would be nice to have somewhere beautiful though.

What time is Aziza out and about? Did wonder if I should discuss letter with Maddy – a bit scared of sending now, it's very raw. X

Email from Robin, 8.58am

Hi! Yes, quite capable of demonstrating nuttiness. And you're right – definitely run your letter by Maddy – she does have wisdom, I think. And there is absolutely no need for me to get it today. The place is a bit of a challenge (though of course relative to our other challenges it is sort of a luxurious one – if you get what I mean). x

Email from Susannah, 9.08am

Yes a much easier challenge – although at the moment I can over-think anything!

I wonder if you might be ON THE INTERNET for a little while A is out ... X

Email from Robin, 9.26am

Yes, I can be. It will be somewhere around 11.00. x

Email from Robin, 10.03am

Aziza outing cancelled! I can speak briefly – and we will probably want to confer post Maddy. A. goes home tomorrow morning and then I am free to focus fully. Although I do have a long-standing commitment on Wednesday; and a doctor's appt. 12 noon, Thursday. X

I sit on top of a hill – it's a good place to have a crisis – and I talk to Maddy on the phone. I feel like I can't breathe. I'm not sure I have breathed all weekend.

I send Maddy my 'serious' email; in what may be the understatement of the year, she agrees it may be 'a bit much' to send to Robin at this stage, and I tell her I really, really want to meet Robin as soon as possible – to get all this out of my head and somewhere that looks a lot more like reality.

Robin

Just had a phone call from Maddy to arrange the time and place of our meeting. I had been gearing up for a meeting in about a week's time, or the coming Friday possibly, at the earliest.

Maddy: Susannah can't do Friday. What about Thursday?
Me: Oh, dear, I have something on then that I can't change.

119

Maddy: I'm not available Wednesday, so the only other day possible this week is Tuesday. After that it would have to be next week. Probably better sooner than later.
Me: Tomorrow?! No, that's too soon. I'm planning to get my hair cut ... do other things ... I definitely can't do Tuesday ...

Hi Robin, I'm Susannah

Robin

It's Tuesday – and I'm getting ready to meet Susannah.

I have to say, I am quite good at sudden about-turns and back-downs. Many a time I have said 'I can't, I won't' – only to find myself doing the thing a very short time later. At least I am adaptable.

We are to meet at the National Gallery, a good compromise between Susannah's need for open space (diffuse the pressure, the ability to escape if necessary?) and my preference for contained privacy (consistent with my need to fully concentrate, sharpen the focus, pin down reality as it were).

So, somewhere between a cell and a paddock.

Susannah

Tuesday, 6 am. I run along the beach hoping I can run even some of the adrenalin out of my body, loosen even one nerve or quieten and exhaust one racing thought. The mission is not completely successful, but it fills in an hour. Seven and a half to go.

The morning passes, glacially. I take Emma to school, complete robotic email processing and pretend to work, appointments pass

121

and then here we are. Time to get ready. Nearly fifty years on, it's time to meet my birth mother. And the obvious question hangs: what do I wear?

It's like dressing for a date – how am I supposed to look? Not too smart, not too try-hard, not like a work thing but not too casual either, and not too I-just-came-from-the-gym-and-this-doesn't-really-mean-anything. Somewhere in the middle, something I feel comfortable in, that's just me. But what is that?

I churn through options in my head with an increasingly dry mouth and an ever more frantic dancing in the tummy, and resist the recurring impulse to call in sick and give the whole thing up, to leave it in the realm of a nice romantic idea rather than confront what might be a messier reality.

I send a selfie of proposed clothes to Em. 'Yes, wear that, it's you, Mum,' comes the confident reply from the wise woman stuck in the teenage body.

I buy flowers – it's a weird kind of Mother's Day after all – and pack some of the photos Maddy has suggested, then take my heart out of my stomach and head down St Kilda Road towards the gallery.

The plan is simple: meet Maddy first outside the National Gallery of Victoria, and then meet Robin in the beautiful and spacious hall. The need for openness and somewhere of beauty loomed large. Openness or escape? I wasn't sure, but it was definitely not going to be in a confined, ugly public-service office.

Robin

I get dressed: black trousers (*Roro*, I hear my six-year-old grand-daughter say in my mind, *why do you always wear black trousers?*), a shirt and a cardigan – the same one I was wearing in the photo I sent to Susannah. I have misgivings, now, that that photo was too flattering. I liked it and chose it for that reason, of course, but wasn't it a deception? And now the reveal! In reality I look older: lined face, saggy neck. How absurdly superficial of me, at seventy-two to be thinking of my physical appearance! I don't really care, but a tiny part of me does, it seems.

I'm not really nervous, just incredibly excited. I tell Matilda: 'Guess where I'm going today? Into the city to meet Susannah.' 'No!' she says in disbelief.

I feel the same: how can this be? Is it actually happening? This, too, is like a dream, but in the sense of it being too good to be true. A miracle.

I catch the train to Flinders Street.

Susannah

At 1.45pm, I park the car in St Kilda Road – how much money do I put in the meter? Two hours? Three? I put in coins to take me up to 9pm – go figure – and I walk, feeling increasingly sick, towards the gallery.

The water flowing down the front of the gallery is one of life's simple joys. Child or adult, I love the slight wrongness of sticking your hand in the cascading water. I have to do it every time we go past; it's a thing.

So, I do it again, looking towards the gallery entrance as I do. The closed gallery entrance. The closed-on-Tuesdays gallery entrance. My perfect plan is in tatters. I contemplate running back to the car.

Except here comes Maddy, who arrives bang on 2pm – the only part of the plan that works. A cunning Plan B is hastily built between us: I will find an equally beautiful place across the road at Federation Square, not quite the same vision but … and Maddy will intercept Robin and I will call her and tell her where I am. Excellent, we are back on track. Ish. We set off across the bridge.

And then.

Birth mother at twelve o'clock. I see Robin, wearing the same cardigan as in her photo, walking towards us. This is so not the plan. Before she spots me, we move to Plan C. I reel off to the right to Fed Square while Maddy moves to meet Robin. I look for any place that might vaguely fit the criteria of 'lovely' along the riverside walk: perhaps flowing water, a wooden bench under a tree and away from the crowds, the odd swan gliding by. Calm beauty.

Robin

I set off across Princes Bridge towards the gallery. A young woman comes up to me: 'Robin?' Of course, it must be Maddy – but she's so young! Not the mature woman I envisaged behind the gentle, wise voice on the telephone. What a good job she does. (It's also a good job that I am wearing my identifying cardigan, because, for some crazy reason, I have my mobile phone turned off and she needs to inform me that the gallery is closed and we are relocating to Federation Square.)

Crossing St Kilda Road, Maddy, remembering my flusterings the day before, kindly reassures me: 'Your hair looks nice.' Despite the fact that she is young enough to be my daughter, I am definitely the child right now, and Maddy is my security object.

Susannah

It's hopeless. Abort Plan C, bin it along with Plans A and B. My intention of finding a lovely calm meeting point is obliterated by the rubbish floating past in the river, noisy school kids and the cleaning truck blowing dust in my face. I look up the riverside walk and see Maddy and Robin walking towards me.

I could just run now and ring later.

Or not.

Not. Bugger it, forget the plans. Maybe the vision is overrated.

I stand in the middle of the crowded path, people milling either side, and awkwardly holding my bags in both hands. With my heart in my mouth, I walk up to them.

'Hello, Robin, I'm Susannah.'

We hug.

Now what?

Robin

We both rise to the occasion, countering awkwardness with humour, and the three of us proceed to find somewhere to have a coffee.

Our default venue, a rather bleak, nondescript little cafe, is unideal, but unimportant at this point; Maddy, on the other hand, is very important in her role as reassuring buffer.

Drinks are procured, photos are shown and we chat – quite comfortably, I feel.

Susannah

The cafe is a long way from my vision of beauty but what can you do? We sit down and both look at Maddy, like two schoolkids waiting for the teacher to tell them what to do.

Luckily she does. She suggests we show each other the photos we have brought. We obey, and conversation slowly starts then keeps going, with the odd nudge from Maddy when too long a pause arises. It's not that there's nothing to say, it's more that there's everything to say and I am struggling to stop staring at Robin, and taking in that I came from her. To say it is weird is an understatement, yet the slowly building momentum of the conversation pulls us along.

After an hour Maddy leaves Robin and me alone for thirty minutes as it was agreed she would. The plan is that when she returns she and I will leave Robin and go somewhere else to quietly reflect on what has happened. Maddy had thought two hours was the perfect amount of time for the first meeting.

But the plan goes to pot. Maddy returns and we tell her we've decided to stay longer. Maddy looks at me, rather penetratingly I feel, possibly trying to sign with her eyes that this is not my most brilliant idea. I look back at her with, I hope, equally meaningful eyes: *It's all good, I've got this.*

Robin

Maddy leaves and Susannah and I decide it's time to perhaps seek a more congenial environment. However, this is not to be so easily afforded us. As we step outside, the weather, which has wavered all day between good and bad, suddenly opts for horrific and unleashes an icy wind and torrential, driving rain.

It really is ghastly: I am freezing, tottering precariously over the slippery cement paving of Federation Square, my head bowed against the elements, my precious hair now fully embracing drowned-rat mode.

Susannah jokes, 'This is not good – I'm going to kill my birth mother on our first meeting!' Believing it to be not altogether outside the bounds of possibility, I half-laugh, half-sob, as I stumble on.

Susannah

I leave Robin on the windswept but vaguely dry stage of Federation Square and head off to Flinders Street station to buy an umbrella. Is nothing going to go to plan?

Robin

I watch her go, much as one might have watched the doomed Oates set out into the Antarctic blizzard. But she does return and, armed with the umbrella, we embark on the last leg of what I have come to regard as our 'ordeal'.

But lo – the beckoning light of a Southbank restaurant! We enter, dripping, and find a table looking out on to the river. The place is peaceful, warm and, of course, dry. I feel I am in paradise.

We order a glass of wine, a platter of antipasto, and settle in. We talk happily for the next two-and-a-half hours. Finally, we have reached our perfect meeting place – but what we went through to get here! Could it be a metaphor?

Susannah

We're dry and it's beautiful looking out over the damp twilight. Finally the vision for our meeting is realised.

It's weird, though. We keep looking at each other, trying to take it, and each other, in. There are gaps in the conversation but they are not uncomfortable. We exchange phone numbers and, when Robin struggles slightly with the technology, I take her phone with a surprising confidence and key in my number. She doesn't seem to mind.

Eight hours after we first met, we part.

Where next? I wonder.

Robin

Out the window, the sky, the river and the city skyline opposite us are suffused in a soft, ethereal light, which over the course of the evening changes from gold, to rose, to blue. It is strangely beautiful – as is this whole thing. That I should be sitting here with my daughter, Susannah, is a wonder and a blessing for which I am profoundly grateful.

V

RIDING THE
ROLLER COASTER

ABBA to the rescue

Susannah

For our second meeting, two days later, we have decided to have lunch at the Botanical Gardens. The original vision of some-where beautiful, somewhere open, is finally going to be realised. There are still some butterflies fluttering in my tummy but this time they are more excited than nervous: I am really looking forward to seeing Robin again.

That morning, doing my exercises (as part of my spasmodic must-not-be-fat-at-fifty campaign) I listen to an ABBA song, 'The Name of the Game'. I am fairly convinced that there is an ABBA song for every key moment in one's life – and this one is the one for this moment. The song is about two people who have only just met, yet seem to get each other. Agnetha (the blonde; I always wanted to be Anni-Frid, the brunette) sings of how this person just seems to understand her, see her and make her open up in a way she hasn't expected. The person's voice and smile make her feel completely at home yet she worries that if she tells the person she cares, that person might laugh or reject her. And so she wants to understand why, what the name of the game is.

Now, really, what is ABBA doing in my mind?! The song

perfectly sums up both the speed with which I seem to have been
hooked, and my fear that it's all going to go wrong. I download
the song on to my phone, thinking I will play it to Robin when we
meet for lunch. It seems a brilliant idea at the time, it will take her
right to how I am feeling. And so, belting the song out as I drive,
I set off for the Botanical Gardens.

This time everything works: it's a beautiful early Spring day,
the gardens are open, daffodils are popping out all over the place, we
both arrive when we say we will, and we head off for a coffee by the
lake. We walk and we talk. We ask and answer questions in an easy,
often amusing exchange with few pauses, none of them awkward.
Robin seems almost unreasonably interested in pretty much everything I say, which is gratifying and makes me talk more, babbling
on about childhood, work, family and, inevitably, ABBA ... which
leads me to my brilliant idea.

'Robin, can I play you a song?'

'A song?' she asks, looking a little confused.

'An ABBA song,' I reply as if that explains everything.

'Here?' she asks, confusion not clearing. 'A song?'

The obvious unspoken words are a seventy-year-old version of
'What the ...?'

Yet I persist, oblivious to the warning signs.

'I'm not very musical,' she says.

'That doesn't matter. It's more the words ...' I say, getting out
my phone.

'Oh, okay.'

I suggest she sits down. She dutifully obeys and I walk away
so she can listen in peace, I believe, to the obvious cut-through
wisdom of the super-Swedes. I am thinking this is good. I am
deluded.

I look back to see her, poor thing, hunched over, my phone to
her ear, straining to hear. And then she is looking quizzically at
the phone, her fingers tapping a little desperately on the screen.

She has, in what I will come to learn is a signature trait, flicked the screen off and has no idea how to get the music back. But, poor, lovely woman, she keeps trying. I can't bear it, it's too painful to watch and I have to intervene. I walk back to the bench.

'Did you listen to it?'

Robin looks a little crestfallen. 'I listened for a little, it was a bit hard to hear the words and then something happened,' she said apologetically.

My brilliant idea is dead in the water.

'It's okay,' I say, conceding defeat and taking my phone. 'Let's go have some lunch.'

Robin

It's a beautiful day and Susannah and I are having lunch at a restaurant on the edge of the Botanical Gardens. We sit outside in the courtyard under a spreading fig tree, surrounded by herb and vegetable gardens with an espaliered fruit tree adorning the wall opposite us. All is delightful.

Susannah is such a good girl, looking after me and attentive to my needs. She is so open and eager to share herself with me. It was disarming of her to bring the ABBA song especially for me to listen to – a pity I really couldn't hear the words at all. I know she feels that she's the needy one in our relationship, the vulnerable one, in danger of putting herself out there and maybe being rejected again, but it's not all one-sided, I have my vulnerabilities too. What if her exuberant and voracious puppy love is just that, something that can subside as suddenly as it came? Lines from *Romeo and Juliet* come to mind: 'It is too rash, too unadvised, too sudden.' In other words, a flash in the pan.

Emotions are unpredictable. Who is more reliable: the one who *feels* she will always stay and love, or the one who has *decided* she will always stay and love?

Over coffee, I try to voice these thoughts.

'Do you think that your feelings for me are in part a bit mixed up with your grieving for your mum? I sometimes think that it may be an emotional flurry that will burn itself out and then you'll say, "I've got that out of my system, I can move on now. Goodbye!"'

Susannah assures me that her mum and I are quite separate – that she has sorted that out and that she doesn't think our relationship is short-term.

That's a good answer and while it doesn't take away all my apprehensions, I'm happy for it and, anyway, right now, under this fig tree, we are enjoying one another, appreciating one another. Both of us, I'm sure, are looking ahead with more faith than fear.

Susannah

Lunch was lovely, more easy talk and laughter but also some deeper moments including Robin voicing some of her fears about our relationship. It's kind of nice not to be the only needy one.

But now the restaurant is closing. We leave and sit outside on a bench in the fading sunlight of the day. Even I, eight hours later, know it's time to go. We walk towards Robin's car and, as we do, I take her arm. She looks taken aback but I don't take my hand away.

'Is that okay?' I ask.

'Yes,' she says. 'It's fine.'

I've never been a fan of 'fine' but I hold my ground and her arm until we get to her car. As she drives away, I realise I am missing her already.

Robin

Alone in my car, I mentally review the day. Our reunion is still a wonder to me; I am so happy. I realise, however, that I am quite emotionally retarded in some areas, particularly in showing physical affection. When Susannah took my arm, I was startled, and felt awkward, out of my comfort zone. Growing up, our family was big on uninhibited verbal communication, but inhibited when it came to physical demonstrativeness. My mum and dad loved me but they were not huggers, and to this day I cannot hug my sister, Susan, with whom I am very close, without feeling awkward. Hugs of convention to relative strangers are not a problem – it's the intimacy that makes it difficult. I am better with little people, my children when they were small and my grandchildren, but it's a slow process of liberation. A young friend from church, Xali, perceiving my constriction in this area, appointed herself my 'hugging coach' and, espousing the pedagogical method of habituation, virtually forced me to hug and be hugged to an alarming extent. Judging by my reaction today, her work is not yet complete.

Over-thinking feeling

Susannah

Normally, ABBA is my happy place but now at least 'The Name of the Game', added to my high-rotation playlist, seems to fuel my over-thinking. Or is that my over-feeling?

There's a lot happening in my life outside this crazy reunion ride: my son is finishing school and then leaving for London, my daughter is leaving for a school exchange in Sweden, Oskar has started his own business and I am launching a new book series. Big milestones are being reached for both parents and children and it's exciting and sad and happy-making all at the same time. Emotions are running high everywhere and no amount of meditation is calming my monkeys.

Because there's so much going on in both our lives, Robin and I won't be able to meet up much in the next fortnight and that, strangely, causes me to fret. We speak a lot on the phone and, again strangely, simply hearing her voice seems to calm the sense of panic that is rising up in me these days. There's this constant tension between excitement and fear and I really struggle to manage it.

I write both professionally and personally, but I have never written poetry before. Yet now, the control and precision it demands seems exactly what I need to try to make sense of what is going on.

So, I sit down and try to write and wrangle this moment. Finally, I get this, and I send it to Robin.

> Hurtling, hurt, towards something light
> Open, opening, something dark
> Scaring, soothing, healing, hurting
> Soaring, sinking, blocking, blurting
> Towards an unknown, fiercely felt home

She replies in an email:

That is so moving, so impressive.

I love you very much. I want to be worthy of you.

See you tomorrow.
Xxx

I am overjoyed with this response. I reckon this poetry thing has a lot going for it.

Heed the carousel

Robin

I see an article in *The Age* newspaper about a new art installation at the National Gallery. It is a golden carousel, set up in the main foyer, that you can actually ride on. This captures my imagination at once. The carousel is beautiful to look at, all in gold (or brass, really), with mirrors and delicate little swinging chairs. What a poetic, whimsical concept: a merry-go-round in an art gallery.

And it is just the sort of thing for Susannah and me to experience on one of our outings. I can see us whirling round and round, gathering speed, the chairs swinging out to the side as we go. Exhilarating – as is the whole adventure we are on: getting to know each other, delighting in our shared sense of humour, the click of connection.

Susannah agrees it's a good idea, so one fine morning, we head off to the gallery.

And there is the carousel, in all its glory, in the large foyer. A small crowd stands around it, while some people are already seated on it, waiting for the ride to start. We think we might watch from the sidelines before taking our turn, but as nothing seems to be happening, we approach the attendant and ask when the next ride is due to start. Then comes the deflating disclosure: it has already begun. In fact, it has never stopped, it is just that the rate of motion is so slow, it is barely perceptible to the eye. Looking more carefully, we discern that the passengers are not entirely static, and one can join their number at any point, as there is clearly little risk of injury either boarding or alighting from the all but stationary vehicle.

Reluctantly letting go of our giddy vision of whirling golden chairs (which, on reflection, given the limited space, may have endangered bystanders), we decide we will go on it anyway, adjusting our mindset from madcap to meditative. We take our seats and sway our way restfully around the circuit at a snail's pace. We have been brought to heel, forced to settle down and attempt Buddhist mindfulness. We stay for three revolutions before deciding we need a little more action. Having alighted, we are henceforth numbered among the enlightened ones, guides and mentors to others. Overhearing a father encouraging his little daughters, telling them that soon the merry-go-round ride will start, not long to wait now, I am able to disabuse him of his misconception, gently informing him that what he is looking at now is as good as it gets.

Over coffee, we jokingly concede that we may have been given a sign, yea, even a warning? *You need to slow down*, says the hidden voice. *Too much speed will end in tears.*

Round and round the garden

Susannah

We retreat to the gallery cafe to recover from the non-existent whirl of the carousel.

I get our coffee, we sit, and the conversation moves a bit lurchingly but the amusement of the non-moving carousel keeps the mood light. As I talk and gesticulate with my hands, my hand brushes Robin's and it makes me feel something. I feel like I want to hold her hand.

Is that weird? I do it with my friends, and my family obviously. It's a connecting, warming thing, but perhaps it's weird here, now? Perhaps it will just come over creepy? Then I remember when I hugged Maddy goodbye last week, Robin commented that I seemed to like to hug a lot: did that imply that she did not? Probably. I think, *Maybe don't take her hand, it will definitely play creepy.*

'Let's go,' I say and we head out to another exhibition in the gallery gardens, where a 'perfume sensory experience' is being held. It's not brilliantly signed but little booths dot the garden, so we head off to the first one. We put our heads into the booth. We are not overwhelmed by smell: actually we can't smell anything.

But there is a light spray to our left – perhaps that is the sensory experience? It's quite beautiful really, the spray twinkling in the sunlight, the smell floating over the garden bed. We put our heads into the spray and there it is – a refreshing, quite floral aroma. It's a bit wet, but beautiful. This is brilliant and we look, eagerly, for the next one. We approach the next flowerbed and again put our heads – and now awakened noses – into the spray. It seems rather similar to the last smell but perhaps that is our uneducated noses letting us down? We go in again trying to pick up a difference – ah yes, this one is more grassy, isn't it? Less floral? We are getting the hang of this thing; we are probably brilliant, we are definitely impressed with ourselves.

And then a well-dressed woman approaches us. We have probably lingered too long in our new olfactory experience, we think; time to let other people enjoy it. She moves quite close to us. 'You know,' she says. 'You need to get one of these.' She offers a strip of paper to us.

'Ah,' we say, 'thank you!' thinking this way we won't get so wet. But there was more. 'And then,' she continued, 'you dip it into the small wells in the booths.' 'But it's here,' we politely begin to correct, indicating the garden beds with our wet hands. 'No, it's not,' she even more politely advises. And she was right. We have been smelling the gallery garden's watering system.

We can't stop laughing: surely the grassy-versus-floral aroma was real? (Although we did wonder about the wetness.) And how could we have missed the testing wells in the booths?

We now progress around the booths – where, now we know where to look and smell, there are quite amazing perfumes, far from the common garden variety of our first attempt. We see other people struggling with the exhibition and a few, we are gratified to see, are also strangely drawn to the water sprinklers. With the missionary zeal of the newly converted we move among the unenlightened offering testing strips and showing the way.

Our senses finally sated, we sit outside in the gardens and talk. The gallery will soon close but I don't want to go. I want to stay here. It's easy, it's fun and I feel like staging a sit-in and just not leaving. There's that irrational, ridiculous feeling again, like I'm threatening a tantrum – get a grip, Susannah.

And then Robin moves her chair closer to mine – right next to mine – touching it. I feel like I have won the lottery.

Lamb shanks for $12

Robin

It's Friday night and I'm off to 'the other side' (the eastern suburbs of Melbourne), to meet up with my sister Susan, who had moved to Melbourne in 1985, twelve years after me. Both being single mothers, we have been close companions and confidantes. She also became a Christian, which further bonded us. Tonight we are going to a seminar at our church on inner healing through the love of God. I'm a bit desperate, actually; this whole thing with Susannah has challenged me emotionally and made me aware that I am not really as free in this area as I need to be. I need to ask God to help me, to break me open, to teach me to love.

To escape the harrowing Friday-night traffic, I am going early to Susan's, aiming to get there about 4.30pm in time to watch *The Bold and the Beautiful*, to which we are somewhat addicted. Yes – I must confess it – no secrets, no matter the risk to reputation! The half-hour spent slumped on the couch watching this appalling but addictive show is, I feel, akin to taking a drug that slows down all physical and mental activity to a more-or-less vegetative state. Definitely relaxing.

After that, Susan and I will set off for church, via the Stamford Hotel for our seniors' dinner meal.

Susannah

Robin tells me that she's going to be over my side of town and I jump at the possibility we might meet. Part of me, the grown-up part that has been missing in action a bit lately, thinks Robin has a pretty full afternoon, but that pesky inner child is leaping up and wanting to be included. So, I find myself suggesting that I come to a seniors' dinner that she is off to with her sister Susan. Robin seems surprised that I'd like to do it, but is happy to go with it. We agree to meet at a cafe first and later at a pub near her church for the dinner. I am absolutely not invited to Susan's house for the soap opera in the middle, and I am told I will have to find something else to do for that hour. Unbelievably, I accept these conditions.

Robin

We have our coffees, talk and laugh, and it is lovely as usual; then it's time for the 'Bold'. Susannah says she may as well come and watch it with us because she has nothing else to do before dinner. I really don't want her to come to Susan's place – I am not ready just yet for the full exposure of my shameful soap watching. While Susan – like the rest of my family – is very keen to meet Susannah, I genuinely feel it would be unfair to spring such a visit on her without warning. So, we part company, each to our respective limbos: Susannah condemned to an hour of aimless driving, me to my half-hour of suspended animation.

Susannah

I take Robin to her car and she drives away, a little too quickly perhaps. I feel slightly abandoned and contemplate my next hour. Why on earth did I agree to this? I blame my little friend.

I decide to drive and check out her church. I know very little about it, yet there's something that scares me, possibly because my experience of church is very traditional, I suppose, very quiet. Robin's church sounds more modern, noisier, with the swaying and the shouting and clapping of hands. I don't think I want to know about it, but here I am driving straight towards it.

I drive up into a suburban street, feeling a little ninja-like, and come to the address. There is nothing to see, though, nothing to alarm, just a large box-like building. A little relieved, I reset my sat-nav for the Stamford, wondering what a seniors' meal is.

Robin

In the car park of the Stamford I spot my daughter's blonde, curly head bobbing around the car park, talking on the phone. We get her attention and she comes over to us.

'Susan, meet Susannah.'

They hug and, as they do, I am struck by a definite family likeness, especially in the curly-hair department. We go into the hotel and, on our way through the foyer to the bistro, I look into the gaming room, off to the left. I don't gamble but, as always, the gaudy colours and the flashing lights of the poker machines captivate me – I really find them beautiful. Proust-like, they trigger childhood memories of seaside carnivals and summer holiday nights with my parents in hotel beer gardens with coloured lights, artificial, tropical plants and fruit cocktail drinks striped with layers of different colours (I always wondered how they did that). So strong is the childhood imprint that even today all this remains the epitome of excitement and glamour.

We pass into the bistro, show (sadly, unnecessarily) our proof of seniority, order our meals, take a number on a stick and find a table. Susannah is clearly out of place – a youthful anomaly in a sea of seniors. Perhaps people are wondering what sad set of circumstances has led this attractive young woman to spend her Friday night thus?

Susan and Susannah connect easily. My sister tells me later that she could see no sign in Susannah of the insecurity I had spoken of; she found her witty and confident. The whole occasion is enjoyable in a quaint sort of way. The food, for Susan and me anyway, is excellent value. I can't go past the $12 lamb shanks, which are delicious.

The meal over (always a quick, efficient affair), we pay the bill, bid Susannah goodbye and head off for church.

Susannah

It has been a long time since I have finished dinner by 6.30pm but it was lovely to meet Susan. I sail home to my family on a quiet freeway with both inner child and outer sensible woman feeling content.

Derailment

Robin

Susannah will come to my house for the first time today. It's quite a big deal; I definitely want to make a good impression. Living alone, at least I don't have to worry about getting anyone else out of the way – I have a clear space to prepare for her visit. I busy myself getting the house nice and fuss over what to provide for meals.

For lunch, I have gone for low-key elegance – a delicatessen selection of cold meats, cheeses, salads, good bread. Dinner, if she stays, will also be safe and simple: a good steak and salad, can't go wrong there.

Susannah

I am a little nervous as I drive to Robin's house. I am not familiar with the area (although being a navigational moron, I'm not really familiar with any area) and it's over the other side of town, but I trust in ABBA and my car's navigation system to keep me calm and get me there. I turn into the little court and look for Robin's house. I recognise it immediately from my Google stalking but I notice it is a lot nicer than the picture I found, with a lovely front garden added, including an abundance of passionfruit spilling over a trellis.

I have a little 'hello house' present of an orchid, which I nearly drop as I get out of the car, but I make it to the front door and ring the bell.

'Hello,' Robin says, beaming as she opens the door.

I clumsily thrust the orchid bowl at her rather than graciously offering it and there is a hug of sorts. I come in to her living room and try not to look as if I'm sussing it out but of course I am; I'm looking for clues as to who Robin is.

I lock on to a bookshelf filled with books. Knowing Robin studied English at uni, it doesn't surprise me but I find it comforting; it will be something we have in common. I am a little surprised – heading towards unsettled – when I see that the bookshelf is almost exclusively filled with books about God. I suppose it shouldn't be a surprise – she's been quite open about the strength of her faith – but there are a lot of books. A lot. I also see framed bible readings on the wall, on the shelf and on the fridge, and by the TV is a vase of dried wheat sheaves to which I immediately ascribe some religious meaning. I'm not sure what to say, so I don't say anything, but hope I am smiling.

Robin

Susannah makes no comment on my house, but later says she likes the atrium and the little courtyard garden out the back. We sit out there and talk. And, finally, I tell her the story of my pregnancy and her birth.

I explain about my absurd naivety, the repressed social attitudes of the time and the sense of guilt and shame. I also tell her frankly that I was immature and self-centred and that I had my own idea of how I wanted my life to go; that it was not so much an unwanted baby as an unwanted pregnancy – a much easier thing to terminate, one way or another. I admit this to be wilful blindness, rationalisation, but there it was. I tell her it was all so unreal for me, I was wrapped up in myself, and I was not alive to any maternal feelings.

Looking at Susannah, it's hard to tell what she is thinking or feeling. I can only hope she understands. At least it's out. She can no longer be under the illusion that I was traumatised by having my baby taken from me. I chose to give her up.

I finish talking and Susannah doesn't say anything. Then, quite abruptly, she stands up, mumbling something about wanting to go for a walk, and goes back through the house and out the front door. Through the window, I see her in the garden, looking indecisive and agitated. With a growing sense of alarm, I follow her out.

'Susannah, are you okay?'

She says nothing at first and then asks: 'So, I was never wanted?'

I answer, 'No, not then.'

She turns and walks out into the street. She keeps walking and I watch as she disappears round the corner. It's just as I feared: the truth is out and she is rejecting me.

No, I didn't want her then, but I do now. I have ever since the secret was disinterred in 1989. I want her because she is my child, part of me, although parted from me. We have a blood bond, mysterious but deep and real. But will this be enough for her? Can she forgive me for that original abandonment? Can I make her believe I love her now?

Feeling somewhat numb, I go inside and mechanically set about the task of preparing lunch, unsure who, if anyone, will be eating it.

Susannah

I walk out into the street. I feel hit over the head but not pained, just numb. And I just walk, not sure where I am going but absolutely sure that I need to go. For the first time I get it, it hits me – the realisation that Robin did not want me as a baby.

She did not want me. The story I had been told as a child and believed for nearly fifty years was a fiction. The woman who had me did *not* love me very much – she did not love me at all and she did not want to keep me. I was not taken from her – she gave me up willingly because I was an inconvenience to her life.

What I wrote in my letter to Robin, worrying about how awful she must have felt feeling a baby she would give up kick inside her, was a delusion, a projection. Those feelings of maternal stirrings were mine, not hers – she had had none. I was just a problem to be got rid of.

Pretty much everything I have thought has just been turned on its head: there was no *Love Child* moment, there was no feeling as the baby kicked inside, no regret for what might have been. She wasn't even thinking that she was giving me a better life, only how she could have one. She wasn't thinking of me at all.

There it is, the reality. In that completely ordinary moment, sitting in her garden, it has struck home. For those first days I was not wanted, not loved by anyone at all – anticipated maybe by Mum and Dad, but for ten days not wanted, certainly not loved, not missed, not known. And least of all by my 'mother'. Robin left to return to her life. I was ejected, forgotten, consigned to the stupid 'dream-like trance' she keeps talking about.

Florence Leuba wasn't wanted.

Susannah McFarlane didn't yet exist.

There was only that screaming baby the nurses called Joan Sutherland.

So, now what? This whole little relationship we have been trying to build is untrue – it has been based on false assumptions. I have been so deluded, so wrong – she probably doesn't even really want me now either. Well, I am not going to stay to be rejected all over again.

It has been one hell of a ride, but it is over now. I cannot think how I, we, can possibly get over this, let alone have any kind of relationship.

And then I realise that I have been walking mindlessly and now have no idea where I am. Looking around me, I see I am walking alongside a cemetery – talk about a metaphor. Is my relationship with Robin dead? Probably.

Fuck.

I stop walking. What's the point? If I keep walking I will get lost. So, I sit pathetically under a tree looking out on the grave-stones and try to steady myself.

Ever the optimist, looking for the up-point, I do feel lucky to be alive – were it not for Robin's dream-like trance I would have been aborted. So, at least I'm here, but that's all I have and I feel sad, a really heavy, hopeless kind of sad. And at a complete loss as to what to do next. I really want to go home but I have left my phone and my bag in her house. Bugger, no easy escape. I will have to go back to get them. But how am I going to do that?

Um, just getting my stuff, sorry about lunch, this probably isn't going to work, is it? Um, okay, bye. Or do I not say anything at all, just get my stuff and go? My bag is close to the front door, I could do a grab and dash. Why not? After all, I don't owe her anything.

Is that what I want? I am pretty sure it is, but I also feel rude. She has made lunch.

What the? I've just been told by my birth mother that she had absolutely no feelings for me at all and gave me up without any problem, and I'm worrying about spoiling her lunch. Am I joking? No, it seems not. I'll be polite, no point making a scene. I'll have lunch, as quickly as possible and then leave, go home, don't come back. Ever.

So, I walk back and find Robin's street, turn into her front garden and open the fly-screen door. Robin is in the kitchen, putting lots of little yummy things on plates. Who knows what she is thinking, who knows what I am?

She looks at me, a little anxiously. I soften a little. I can't leave now – it would be too rude. I walk into the kitchen. Robin looks at me and puts her arms up.

'I do love you, Susannah.'

There's an awkward hug. Then we finish preparing the lunch together, both probably grateful for something to do. She had gone to a lot of trouble, chosen a delicious smorgasbord of bread, salad, meats and cheeses. We sit down, we eat and we start to talk. The conversation could not be more awkward to begin with: wooden comments about how lovely the bread is, inane critiques on cheese. But as we continue to talk, there's something about Robin's voice that calms me and the way she looks at me when I talk melts something in me and the conversation warms again. Once again, it seems almost ridiculously easy to share stories, to listen and laugh. I feel listened to and I soften. I stop thinking about how I am going to excuse myself and leave.

Then Robin brings up my birth again, and the same visceral stab of pain returns. She wants to talk about it some more. I don't want to and I bat it away and start talking too much about something I can't even remember. My mind starts racing away again.

What am I doing here? And how do we move on from this?

Like everyone does surely – by watching *The Bold and the Beautiful*.

When Robin suggests it, part of me thinks she's mental but, hey, what's there to lose? I'm up for it. I'm exhausted, I don't want to talk anymore – there's been too much talking, too much thinking, trying to wrangle too much feeling.

We sit side by side on her sofa. Robin is right about the sedative powers of the show. I lean in to her and Robin tentatively puts her arm around me. I fold and give in. I lie down in her lap and she strokes my head.

It could be weird if it wasn't exactly what I needed. The little baby who stormed out of the house, rejected and hurt, has come back and needs to be calmed and comforted. She isn't alone. She is wanted. Now, anyway.

So, we sit on the sofa and something mends as we lie there watching a fashion family dynasty embroil themselves in drama, albeit at a glacial pace.

But I am a bit envious of that glacial pace. We are back from the brink but I feel like I'm on a runaway train and I don't know how to slow it down. And I'm not even sure who's driving it anymore.

Robin

Feeling like we are survivors from some sort of wreck, I suggest we have our evening meal, which we eat outside in the courtyard. The night is calm and mild and we can smell the honey fragrance of the butterfly bush. It is delightful sitting there together. Susannah pronounces the steak tender, the salad tasty – and equilibrium is restored.

When it is time for her to leave, I pick her a bunch of roses to take home.

Are we all right? Is our little boat still afloat?

With all my heart I hope so.

Crawling back

Susannah

I come home from Robin's still slightly shell-shocked.

'How was it?' asked Oskar

'It was good,' I lie as I put Robin's roses in a vase on our back table.

Over the next couple of days, I try to take in what Robin has told me and how that now re-shapes the story that I have told myself about myself all my life. The first chapter obviously needs a massive rewrite and I reckon I need to write it if I am going to be able to have any sort of relationship with Robin.

So, I sit and stew and write another poem.

Heartbeat to heartbeat.
One, then two, then, oops! three.
Fix this, hide this
Dream-like, dispatched, drugged and ripped
3,2,1 Bang! Wake up!
Cut loose, covered up in a crib-cage
Screaming a fury down a cold corridor
This never happened. Bury. Put to sleep. All will be well.
Hole.

Found, felt – finally – held
Layers of gentle, constant love poured into the hole.
Weave a beautiful blanket of carefully chosen strands slowly,
    strongly.
Wrapped round tight. Safe now. Love this one
An ever-vigilant eye watches for cracks, pours more, holds and
    heals, weaves.
But something calls up from deep below.
Too hard, threatening to unravel the hard-won blanket.
Let's dig it down again, kindly we hope, where it can't hurt.
All will be well
Hold on.

And so life goes, everyone walks at least a little wounded.
Calls come from below
A hopelessly blank medical form starts a wonder
A glimpse-seeking Dryburgh Street dash (who me? Curious?
    Not at all …) tilts you downwards
A baby on the breast takes you very close.
Little tugs, pulls at threads.
Holes appear.

And then, in a calm carved out from the storms, something opens.
This time it's allowed out and followed.
New threads weave easily into the blanket with a joyful constant
    clicking.
But the gaping, weeping wound also wakes.
We're on it. Clever words sent swooping to rescue, with a brave
    but horrible honesty, casting, recasting to fix this.
Too many, too much.
Run, retreat, close this, forget this, fuck this.
But can't. Don't want to. Walk back up. Go back inside.
Go home. To her.

But no more words, no more clever. Just be quiet. Go back to
    the start.
Lie down, back together, open. Heartbeat to heartbeat.
Bold, beautiful. All will be well. Wonderful.
Keep crawling back to
Whole.

I decide to take the poem to Robin rather than just email it, but I'm a little scared about how she will react. I'm worried that she will be angry about my being angry, upset that I am upset, and that she might decide I'm too much hard work, not worth the effort. After all, it's only three weeks since we met.

On the way to her house, I think I might buy Robin a bunch of roses to go with the poem. I hope that might help: soften the blow, maybe. I am telling her that she has hurt me and I buy her flowers? That's messed up, isn't it?

I stop and buy the flowers.

Robin

Susannah is at my door with a bunch of white roses. I exclaim over them, how beautiful they are, and go to find a suitable vase. We sit on the couch and she tells me she has brought me something else – a poem she has written.

'Do you want to read it?' she asks.

'Of course I do.'

It is an amazing poem; she writes with such beauty and clarity. And what is clear is that she really does finally get it – the truth that I knew she had to get, that I wanted her to get even though I feared the outcome. She had not been wanted; she had not been welcomed into the world by her mother. How terrible; I start to cry.

'Susannah, I'm so sorry for hurting you, for deserting you. Can you forgive me?'

'Yes,' she says.

I am so grateful for her courage and willingness to keep follow-ing after love, despite the pain. I know she wants to forgive me; I hope that deep down she really has.

Susannah

I feel better having shared the poem with Robin. I said I forgave her. Somehow, I thought it would be harder.

VI

TAKING REFUGE

Longleaf – 1

Susannah

Robin, the reunion, everything has been doing my head in and, I suspect, hers. I feel we need to get away, spend some time away from the demands of our families and just focus on trying to get this relationship, if that's what we are calling it, on to some sort of even keel.

I ask Robin if she would like to come up and stay for a few nights at Longleaf, our farm. She is at first reluctant, then unsure, but finally agrees. I am happy for that. I plan what I hope she will think are nice meals, buy a teapot for her morning tea and pack my adoption folder and some photo albums from when I was little, which Robin has asked me to bring. Then, on a beautiful spring morning, feeling both excited and a little anxious, I pick Robin up from her house and we drive to Longleaf.

Robin

On our first afternoon at Longleaf, sitting together in the sun on a wooden bench away from the house, with a view down the hill to meadows and gum trees, Susannah shows me her adoption folder.

It gives me a shock to see my 23-year-old handwriting on letters I had written from Perth to the social worker in Melbourne.

Do I know the girl behind that small, immature script? Does she have any connection with me now?

Then I read the Form of Consent; I look at my crimped little scrawl, signing away, sight unseen, my child, and something gives way. From some contained, interior sea, tears leak out through the cracks in the stone fortress; but the structure holds.

FORM 4

FORM OF CONSENT BY PARENT TO ADOPTION ORDER

IN THE MATTER of the Adoption of Children Acts

and

IN THE MATTER of FLORENCE LEUBA
an infant

I, ROBIN ISABEL LEUBA the undersigned, of

being the mother ~~father~~ (1) of the above-named infant, who was born at EAST MELBOURNE

VICTORIA on the 14TH day of JULY 1965 .(2)

hereby state:—

  1. That I understand the nature and effect of an adoption order for which application may be made.

  2. That in particular I understand that the effect of such order will be permanently and totally to deprive me of my parental rights in relation to the above-named infant.

  3. That I hereby consent to the making of an adoption order in respect of the said infant.

  4. That I further understand that this consent may be withdrawn by me upon the following conditions but not otherwise:—

     (a) That within thirty days of the giving of this consent I sign a revocation thereof in the form or to the effect of the form set out hereunder; and

     (b) that within seven days of the signing of such revocation I deliver it or by registered letter post it to the Registrar of the County Court, Law Courts, Melbourne.

IN WITNESS WHEREOF I have signed this consent on the 21ST

day of JULY , 1965 , at CARLTON

Signature: *Robin Leuba*

SIGNED in the presence of —

Signature:

Address: ROYAL WOMEN'S HOSPITAL, CARLTON

Occupation: MEDICAL SOCIAL WORKER

Susannah

It's weird showing Robin the adoption folder. She doesn't seem to remember much at all and seems genuinely surprised when she sees copies of the letters both she and her mum had written to arrange the adoption. It was indeed, as she had said, as if she had buried everything deep, deep down. Forgotten.

Then Robin reads the Form of Consent. She looks up, eyes tearing a bit.

'I feel sad,' she exclaims.

I run to get some tissues from inside but by the time I get back, she seems to have recovered, and is on to the next page, declaring the whole thing 'amazing'.

That's it? I wonder. *That's the reaction?*

The rest of the afternoon passes easily – Longleaf is a beautiful place to just be – and we eat an early dinner and watch *Mamma Mia*, the ABBA movie with the ability to heal all pain. Robin seems to enjoy it, so that's a good sign: I do judge people on how they react to ABBA.

Robin goes to bed but I stay up a bit longer. I'm tired, it's been a big day, but I feel rattled again, this now too familiar feeling of upset and slight panic creeping up on me. I hate it, it messes things up and is too much – too much feeling, unprocessed and raw but powerful – too powerful for me to handle. It seems Robin is not the only one who has buried stuff, but my stuff seems to have no problem coming out and beating me up, determined to be heard and felt.

So I sit, sipping my wine, a baby Buddhist, trying to watch the feeling come and swirl and hoping I can then watch it go again. But tonight the feeling of sadness persists and pulls at me and I can't shake it. A tear falls, again. Get a grip, Susannah – it's been a good day, just calm down, it's all okay.

But it's not. I feel sad, really sad, the same heavy sadness I felt at Robin's house. Looking through the adoption folder and my baby photos with her has taken me back again to that abandoned baby and now her sadness is swelling up in me, building like a huge wave.

What am I going to do with it? I have one thought on what I could do, but I immediately dismiss it. It's dumb. No way. I'm not doing that.

But then it's back, this time with a rationale. Why wouldn't you wake Robin up and tell her? You're sad because of what happened, what happened with her so, why not tell her?

Because, I tell myself, trying to wrest some control, because she has gone to bed. Because she is my guest. Because she is old and because, actually, I don't really know her. It's embarrassing. I can't just unload on her like this, show that much vulnerability.

But the other voice is persistent: aren't you here to deal with this stuff? And she's not just a house guest, is she? She's your birth mother. What are you going to do in the morning? 'Morning,' she'll say, 'did you sleep well?' And you'll say, 'No I didn't, I cried thinking about me as a baby, the baby you left, but I didn't want to wake you, you know, not your problem.'

But it is her problem, isn't it? If this thing is going to go anywhere don't we have to go to the hard places? How can we have a future if we don't look at the past, however painful, together?

So, I take a deep breath, get up and go and knock on her bedroom door.

'Robin?'

No answer. She's asleep. Okay, there's your sign: it is a terrible idea. Close the door, quickly before she wakes up.

'Robin?' I say a little louder.

Robin

I wake and become aware of Susannah standing at my bedroom door saying my name. She is clearly upset. She says she needs to be with me: the little child coming into Mummy's bed.

161

How can I refuse her? I take her in, put my arms around her – and she breaks wide open. The tsunami of her sadness and longing has no trouble sweeping away the barricades of adult reserve and etiquette, and she cries and cries and cries until she is empty.

Even in my tired and taken-off-guard state, I am not such a fool as to not recognise that this is a serious watershed moment; how I respond to it is crucial to the future of our relationship.

But the situation is very challenging. Although at heart our reunion is the redemption of a lost mother-and-baby connection, on the surface now Susannah is not the newborn baby I gave away; we are – on one level and at this point – two adult strangers. Add to this my awkwardness with showing physical affection, and it is doubly difficult. But I do deeply feel the pain of her loss and abandonment and I want to comfort her. So I cuddle her, speak soothing words, and fetch a glass of water and tissues for her runny nose. I do my best, but it's a bit like jumping into a river to save someone while wearing a lead suit.

My poor baby, trying to get blood out of a stone, and haemorrhaging on the stone. It's painful for both of us.

But I do love her.

Susannah

I don't know how long I cried for. I didn't think that was going to happen and it was pretty weird. All the sadness of that baby just burst out of me. The intensity scared me: it was as if I, grown-up normal me, had been swallowed up in a darkness of tears and I couldn't stop. And at times I could hardly breathe.

I remember Robin comforting me (what if she hadn't? That would have finished us!). And I remember she got up a few times, to get more tissues, to fetch me a glass of water. I remember feeling exhausted; at some point I must have fallen asleep.

When I wake up, I'm still exhausted and now also embarrassed, yet there's a palpable sense of lightness. Something has been let out, let go, that clearly needed to be let out but I still don't quite know what to make of it. Do I apologise? No, I don't think I did anything wrong – confronting definitely but not wrong. Instead I decide to thank her.

Longleaf – 2

Robin

The next morning, Susannah brings me a cup of tea in bed – something I will never cease to covet and appreciate. She sits on the side of the bed to drink her coffee and it is all very companionable and easy.

But something in me is still un-eased. My heart does want to express how sorry I am for causing her such hurt, for not wanting her back then, neither in the womb nor out of it. I badly want to be able to pour some ointment into those wounds in her soul and spirit.

Susannah

Robin enjoys her breakfast and I enjoy the return to more normal-person behaviour. I am a little anxious to make light conversation, so I begin a discussion of the importance of getting the butter-to-vegemite ratio right (that's me, tackling the big issues head-on) before there's a slightly heavy silence. I'm looking for a bridge back.

Then Robin speaks.

Robin

Jesus is the only person I know who I believe can really heal our wounded souls. So, I ask Susannah if I can pray for her, with her.

Susannah

No, that wasn't what I was thinking of in terms of a bridge. I really did not see that one coming.

'What do you mean?' I ask. 'Do I have to do anything?' I hope not, I really hope not.

'No, just be with me.'

Phew.

'And only if you want to, Susannah.'

No, I don't want to. Of course I don't want to. I feel like I'm about to be initiated into something. It's going to be weird and confronting, isn't it, but – and of course this is the big but – will it be any more weird and confronting than my waking her up, crying half the night and wanting her to comfort me?

I can't possibly say no. It would be rude. No, that's not even it. It's not a manners thing. She is showing me who she is, something that's important to her and she's taking a risk, just like I did. I need to say yes.

Robin

Susannah agrees and I hold her as I go back to the beginning, asking God to bless that un-blessed conception, pregnancy and birth; to redeem and heal. I thank Him for her childhood, for her parents, for who she is now.

As I talk to my Father, pour out my heart to Him for both of us, my tears flow unrestricted, as if drawn up through an artesian well that has been sunk deep, deep down into the earth, opening up a direct line to my heart.

165

Susannah

At first I feel uncomfortable. I close my eyes – am I blocking or concentrating? A bit of both maybe. It *is* weird, it is unsettling, but Robin is so brave and honest. She speaks with such clarity and openness and love. When she cries, I cry too. It is much, much more beautiful than it is weird.

And then she finishes. I tell her it was beautiful and I go to make the tea and coffee.

The rest of the morning is easy, relaxed, fun. We talk – and we talk so easily – and laugh. Topics range widely and change quickly, there is a verbal play that flows easily and delights.

Is it easy because of what has happened or in spite of it? I'm not sure but for now I also don't care – for the morning we can just enjoy the ease of the conversation, the connection, without over-thinking, over-feeling, over-anything.

Robin

This rather extraordinary night and morning have, I think, been cathartic for both of us. We can move more freely and lightly into the new day – starting with breakfast and, of course, more tea!

Susannah

Robin and I seem to have reached a place of calm, in a bubble containing just the two of us. But, of course, it isn't just the two of us: there are many other people who are about to join this reunion and, as we return home, this will be the start of something completely different.

VII

THE RIPPLE EFFECT

All in together?

Robin

Precious and important as our time at Longleaf has been, I am keen for Susannah to integrate with the wider family. For me, the story of our reunion has always been about making things real (both mentally and emotionally), as opposed to dreamlike, and I feel that integration will help achieve this. I want to normalise the situation and establish the validity of Susannah's place as one of my children – like taking the new plant out of its pot and planting it in the permanent garden. Acknowledging my four girls: each one unique and wonderful and secure in her right to belong.

Actually, this inclusiveness has been my vision from the moment I reconnected with Susannah – to gradually (who am I kidding?) gather everyone in the extended family in to welcome and enjoy her return. It is a vision that has its roots in early childhood. Around the age of eight, there was one daydream I savoured: I used to picture a huge bed taking up all the floor space of some sort of corrugated-iron shelter, one side of which was completely open to the elements; on this bed I and all my family were snugly ensconced, watching the pouring rain outside and hearing it clatter on the tin roof while we remained dry and cosy. A final element of bliss was added by the fact that we were all feasting on pies and tomato sauce (I'm an Aussie, through and through).

My idea of Heaven has evolved since then but the essence is still the same: everyone I have ever loved all included and together, enveloped in love, joy and peace, safe home, forever.

Susannah

Outside of Oskar and the kids, I have told no one in my family about contacting Robin and have no plans to. I can barely explain what is going on to myself let alone anyone else. In the rare moments where I yank my head out of my reunion bubble, I can see poor Oskar struggling to keep up with my slightly crazed pace and I am scared of how others might react. Also, I reason, if I can just find my balance with Robin I can then deal other people in later, a lot later. But I haven't counted on Robin's family vision …

Robin

My other three daughters have always wanted to meet their lost sister Susannah, and when my niece, Florence, was on her Google mission – Operation Finding Susannah – they were avid recipients of any information unearthed. There were moments of doubt: Anna expressed authenticity concerns on the basis of Susannah's blonde hair ('We are all brunettes, aren't we?'), apparently forgetting the paternal side of things, but they were grassroots disciples of my vision of family inclusiveness.

In an excess of zeal to bring everyone together, I start to pressure Susannah somewhat to cooperate: 'Would you like to look through the family photo albums? No?' 'I just took out these couple of photos – look how much you look like Anna!' 'Look, here's one of Tim's mother – quite a striking similarity, don't you think?'

Poor girl: she is polite but I'm not sure how she really feels about my vigorous integration campaign.

Susannah

I am struggling with Robin's enthusiasm for me to meet other members of her family, and I'm still adjusting to the fact that I am not just meeting Robin, but a whole family.

Robin, though, is persistent in suggesting that I meet my sisters. Sisters. Even saying the plural is weird to me. Two months ago I had one younger sister and an older brother; now I have five sisters and two brothers and I am torn between trying to realise Robin's comprehensive vision of one big happy family and being scared out of my wits about meeting them all.

I tell Robin that I'd like to take things slowly – although slowness has hardly been a signature trait of this reunion – and not meet anyone else yet. She says she understands, but I don't think she can help herself and she continues to press. My ever-present and pesky inner child is keen to please Robin but I can't even contemplate the photo albums, let alone the real people: I am curious, of course, but also a little unnerved by looking at the lives that went on without me. And if I did meet them, what would they all make of me? Would I be welcome or an intrusion, a novelty or an irritation that distracted Robin from her 'real family'? I don't think I want to know, but I do have to do something to stop Robin bringing them up all the time. I reckon if I look at some of the albums that will keep her satisfied for a little while and I can win some more time.

A few days later I am at Robin's house for dinner and I concede. 'Shall we look at some photos?' I ask.

Robin needs no further encouragement. She disappears down her hallway and returns with an armful of albums. 'Which one would you like to start with?' she asks cheerfully.

'Perhaps around the time I was born?' I answer, unsure if that is actually what I want to do, but it is at least chronologically sensible.

And so we sit on the sofa and look at the first album. There are photos of Robin – she's young, obviously, and beautiful. There are photos of her both before and after my birth and there's really no difference; you'd never know anything had happened – well, of course not, that was the plan. There are photos of Tim and photos of Tim and Robin, but I gloss over them – it's all a bit much.

But there is one photo over which I linger: Robin is sitting outside with a dog in the country somewhere. It was taken a couple of years after my birth. Again, she looks beautiful, quite dreamy yet strong at the same time. I look at it with a pang – she looks nothing like me and she looks completely together and at ease. What did I want? For her to look a little sad, a little damaged? Absolutely. But she doesn't and once again it's confirmed that I was as good as dead to her.

I turn the page and Anna appears.

'See, doesn't she look just like you?' says Robin enthusiastically. I have to admit that she does: we share the same jaw-line, the same eye shape if not colour. It's a bit weird: I have never looked like anyone in my family before.

And then Matilda appears. Same square face.

And Tim disappears.

And Andy appears.

And then, awfully, Andy disappears, drowned at a beach. I remember it from Robin's book, but seeing photos of them all on the holiday and even the beach itself makes it more real.

Robin talks about how messy it was – Tim leaving, Andy dying, her struggle to raise two small daughters – and I begin to get a sense of the 'chaos and turmoil' she referred to in one of her earliest letters to me. I can't help but compare it to the calm, stable childhood I had – parents together in the same house for fifty years – and I feel very grateful to Mum and Dad for it. But I also feel strangely unsettled and a bit jealous and that feeling persists as we look through more albums and I see Robin and the girls change over the years. Oddly, I feel both relieved and left out, simultaneously pleased and sorry not to have been there. I start turning the pages more quickly, wanting to get it over with now, but as I turn one page of a later album I am stopped in my fast-turning tracks as I look at a photo of Anna. She is at some kind of school ball; wearing a black strapless dress, she looks almost exactly like I did at the same age. Indeed, there is a photo of me at a college ball, wearing an almost identical black strapless taffeta dress. I tell Robin and she is delighted. I am a little unsettled.

Robin

Although I have been urging Susannah to look through the photo albums, it's quite a peculiar experience when she does so. It's hard for me to identify with that young, attractive dark-haired girl. Is it really me? Who was she? I am not the same person now at all. The phases of my life seem like a series of balloons connected by a string of time and memory, extending through the years.

Susannah and I don't have that string, that line, connecting us. We have no shared memories of the past yet there is a connection, albeit a mysterious one: something deeper, less linear, that still holds. It's the one that makes separated parents and children seek each other out – a bloodline, a primary source that is seemingly not easily annulled.

Susannah and I early sailed away in different directions from each other. Looking at photos and videos of our separate voyages is like postcards from abroad: fascinating; sometimes happy-making; sometimes sad-making – Wish you were here/Wish I was there. But we do have the present and the chance to turn the bloodline into a heartline. I'm not sure how helpful the photo albums are.

Susannah

I try to move through the last album quickly but, I hope, without seeming rude. Robin talks a little about when she became a Christian and I try to move that along as well. Whenever she talks about God or her Christianity I feel uncomfortable; it's as if I'm talking to someone else, not the Robin I am starting and wanting to get to know. It's clearly very, very important to her and I respect that, but I don't want to know about it because I feel it distances her from me. Soon, however, and thankfully, it's time for dinner, which is lovely. The conversation returns to the present and I drive home feeling calmer.

That night, however, I sleep badly with the photos of Robin spinning around in my mind like a B-grade horror movie. Then I dream that Robin is sitting opposite me but her form keeps changing: she blurs from Robin 1965 to Robin present to Robin 1980s and back again and then the dream cuts to Longleaf where I am walking up the drive. As I walk up, Tim, also shape-shifting from his 1965 to his present self, is walking down the drive towards me. Neither of us stops but he stares at me as he passes. I wake up and stay up for most of the night thinking the photo albums were not a good idea.

Clue: having together a mixed garnish (7 letters)

Susannah

I am back at Robin's house and we are sitting in the garden. Robin goes inside and comes back, not, thankfully, with a photo album but with *The Age* newspaper. 'Let's do the cryptic crossword,' she says. 'It's fun.'

Over the years people have tried to teach me how to do cryptic crosswords and have failed – or I have failed them. I have always wanted to understand them, felt that I should be able to but never got there. So, I don't leap at Robin's suggestion.

'I can't do them,' I say apologetically. 'Wanted to but never can.'

'Oh, you just need to learn the clues,' replies Robin, folding the paper at the crossword page and picking up a pen. Clearly we are going to do the crossword. 'You just need to do them with someone for a while. Come on, come over here next to me, you have to see it.'

My heart sings a little at the seating suggestion but also sinks a little that I am about to expose my cryptic thickness.

Clue: having together a mixed garnish (7 letters)

'Right,' says Robin, shifting into a definite teaching mode. 'Let's find an easy one.'

'Oh, yes, please,' I think and possibly say.

And so, Robin slowly introduces me to the clues: words like 'messed' or 'awry' might tell you it's an anagram; 'the old city' will always be 'Ur' and 'Father' often 'pa'; 'extremes' might tell you to take the first and last letter of a word; and then, if all else fails, just look for the word spelled out in the clue.

I nod, I say 'I see' a lot, even when I don't completely, and I wonder how on earth anyone ever remembers all these rules.

'Here,' says Robin. 'Try this one.'

I look, eager to be a good pupil. The clue is 'Pleasant tumble in gale'. Delighted, I spy the word 'tumble'. 'Anagram?' I ask.

'Good!' she says.

I look again. '"Genial"? Anagram of "in gale" meaning pleasant?'

'Brilliant!' she exclaims. 'You're brilliant at these. I knew you would be!'

I lap up the words of encouragement, feeling chuffed.

'Right, this one,' she says next.

I look but this time I draw a blank. 'Um …'

'The same word defines both parts of the clue,' Robin offers.

'Right,' I say, looking again. 'Um, is it …? It's … No, don't know, it's gone.'

Robin looks across at me and with a kind but knowing smile asks, 'Was it ever there?'

Bugger. No, actually, it wasn't but how did she know that? Any embarrassment at being found out is completely overshadowed at my joy in feeling that Robin somehow gets me, understands me.

We continue, working our way – well, more Robin than me – through the crossword and she is right, doing the cryptic is fun and doing it with her even more so. Over the weeks it becomes a thing, our thing, something that we can do together.

Robin

Susannah is, needless to say, a fast learner with the cryptic, hare-like, overtaking her tortoise tutor in expertise in a relatively short space of time. Nevertheless, I retain a couple of tortoise advantages: probably a wider vocabulary (because I am more ancient), and a certain patient, plodding perseverance that does pay off.

For example, when we get stuck, I systematically go through the alphabet, mentally inserting each letter into the blank space in question. As I laboriously intone A ... B ... C ... I sense the impatience and aggravation of the hare. Also, I will have none of her attitude of, *We've got the right answer – do we really have to know exactly why?*, insisting instead that we proceed no further until we have completely worked it out. Thus I am as an anchor to her kite.

Amid the swirling emotional currents of our reunion and family relationships, the cryptic crossword frequently proves to be a billabong of calm, giving us a breather and bonding us together.

Solution: SHARING.

Meeting Matilda

Susannah

Despite resisting Robin's pressure for me to meet her daughters, I Google and check them out on Facebook – it seems only fair as they have all Googled me. And then, taking myself by surprise, I decide to message them. There is something about doing it on my own terms, away from Robin, and a message seems safer than a meeting. And I can still feel that I am trying to deliver on Robin's vision.

Anna, the oldest sister, and her family are working in Vanuatu, so I decide to message the next one down, Matilda. They are all, of course, much younger than me, so the closer in age to me, the more I think we might have in common. Matilda is the one who apparently kept a watch out for me on the public transport of Melbourne (not knowing that in looking for a brunette she was doomed to fail even if fate had brought us together on a tram), so she seems a good place to start. But what do I write to a sister I've never met? I write this:

> Hi – well, this is weird, but no weirder – and kind of wonderful – than everything else about this path Robin and

I seem to be hurtling down. I am hopeless on FB but at least it's a way for us to make contact – I'd like to. Susannah x

I wonder about the 'x' but leave it there – better to be open and warm than not, I reckon.

I send it off late one afternoon and wait, wondering when or if she will reply. I don't have to wait long: Matilda messages back that evening. She sends a long, long message and I send a long, long reply and then we are off, messaging our life stories over the next twenty-four hours – with the same comfort and ease I felt when I was first emailing Robin. The click of connection is instant and just as I am wondering what will happen next, Matilda bursts right through the security bubble of the message and rings my mobile just as Oskar, Emma and I finish dinner.

'Oh, hi Matilda,' I say looking at Oskar and Emma across the table with a dumbstruck expression. Oskar looks even more gobsmacked than me, but a wide smile breaks over Em's face.

'That's so cool!' she says. 'Put her on speaker!'

I decline that invitation and instead move into another room to talk. Disconcertingly, Matilda sounds remarkably like my sister Sophie, which is odd but it colludes in making me feel instantly at home talking with her – and we talk for two hours, including, eventually, a brief session with Emma on speaker phone. There is no getting-to-know-you, polite, warm-up conversation – we hurtle straight to the heart of things. Matilda has, sadly, suffered from illness most of her life and she talks freely about this, as I do about stuff that has happened to me. It is crazy how deep, how honest we go so quickly, and how we use similar expressions and have the same throaty laugh: it is like talking to myself.

'So, when am I going to meet you?' she asks.

'Um, I don't know …' I begin.

'Tomorrow,' declares Matilda.

'Okay,' I reply.

What? I say to myself, but before I can say, 'Actually, I'm trying not to rush into things', we have arranged where and when to meet the next day.

I get off the phone and walk out into the living room.

'I'm meeting Matilda tomorrow,' I say to Oskar.

'You are? What happened to the go-slow strategy?'

'I'm not sure,' I reply.

Matilda and I have agreed to meet at a park near her place – nice and neutral and easy for Matilda, who doesn't drive. I buy chicken sandwiches and a bottle of champagne and then think, *Gift! I need to buy small gift!* But what does one buy a birth sister? I consider many things and settle on a plant. *Perfect*, I think, *something that grows.* Yet the purchase and the over-thinking behind it has meant I am now running late so, with small butterflies in my tummy and some calming ABBA playing in the car, I drive off to the other side of town. The butterflies have grown quite large by the time I arrive, park and walk across the playground towards a woman in a red shirt who, brown hair aside, looks a lot like me.

We exchange nervous smiles but a warm hug and then we sit under a tree and toast ourselves with the champagne. And we talk and talk and laugh. It is lovely and we only stop because I have to get home because Oskar and I are going out. At one point I reply to something she says, ending with 'Don't be silly, my friend.' And there is a pause, an awkward one, and we both know why – because she isn't my friend. She is my sister.

Robin

Even I am amazed at the whirlwind connection that has sprung up between Susannah and Matilda. Although I am a little stunned by the breakneck speed of it all, I am happy at any sign of family integration. However, their relationship does prove to be rather a runaway cart, crashing through fences of restraint and discretion.

Susannah

Matilda and I speak and see each other often over the next two weeks. I am happy whenever I see her name come up on the phone, as it does one afternoon while I am driving to a meeting.

'Susannah, don't be angry at me!'

'Why would I be?'

'Because I've just told Dad, Tim, about you. It just kind of came out.'

'Matilda! You what?' I shout as I pull the car over to the side of the road.

Timidity

Robin

I had been apprehensive about telling Tim of Susannah's reappearance. I think I feared it might stress him out. However, the choice is taken away from me when I learn that Matilda has let the cat out of the bag by mistake. So, I ring him.

'Tim – hi! It's Robin. So, I hear Matilda told you about Susannah? Unbelievable, that girl! Of course I was going to tell you – I was just waiting for the right moment. I wasn't sure how you'd feel about it. How do you feel?'

'I'm delighted!'

'Really? That's great. It's certainly pretty amazing …'

I share more; I tell him that we have met, whom I think she looks like, that she is a well-known author of children's books.

Tim's last words before he hangs up are: 'I'm going to Google my daughter.'

Armed with this happy information, I enthusiastically launch into stage two of Operation All In Together and begin to harass Susannah over the issue of Tim.

'You know, Tim is so happy that you have reappeared. He would love to meet you anytime you feel ready – no pressure, though.'

Susannah

Perhaps oddly, I haven't really thought much about my birth father – either over the years or now. No one ever asks me, 'Do you want to find your birth father?' It is always about my mother. And so it seems to be now.

Of course, once Robin tells me his name I Google him as well and, because he is an actor, he is easy to find. And it is just as easy to see that I have his eyes and his hair, just as Robin has said. That piques my interest, or something else I have been denying, but I still don't want to meet him. Don't want to or am afraid to? Maybe, probably, both, but either way it isn't happening, however hard Robin pushes. And push she does ...

Robin

I think I have found the perfect way to spark Susannah's interest in Tim. I am sure she will appreciate his wit because she has such a good sense of humour herself. I happen to have a copy of a piece he wrote about his stint as a department-store Santa last Christmas, which I find very funny. So, one day, as we are sitting out in my garden again, I try my new tactic.

'By the way, I have a copy of this piece Tim wrote about when he got a job as Santa in a department store last Christmas. Do you want to read it? I think it's hilarious.'

Susannah

Robin is standing in front of me holding out pieces of paper, an article Tim wrote about a job as a department-store Santa. She wants me to read it. She really wants me to read it. Robin cannot praise it enough: it is, it seems, possibly the funniest thing ever written and I will just love it. She is so enthusiastic that it is impossible for me to say no. It's not that I don't want to read it – who doesn't want to read something funny? It's more that I'm not sure I want to meet Tim, on the page or in person. I haven't worked out how I feel about him and I don't know how he feels about me – after all, he never came looking for me. And, I realise, I am having enough problems digesting meeting Robin and Matilda without adding Tim and the rest of Robin's family to my plate. For one of the few times in my life I seem to be advocating a take-it-slowly approach. However, it is clear that this is not a genetic disposition. But, for now, how can reading the piece hurt?

So, I read it and it is funny, very funny, but I don't say that. I'm not sure I'm ready to concede anything – to myself or to Robin – about Tim. And I am mindful that Robin is watching me read it and that she might take any show of enthusiasm as a green light to talk about meeting Tim. I really can't let her lead me into that.

Robin

I watch Susannah as she reads the Santa composition, waiting with tragic excitement for expressions of amusement, and indeed for outbursts of laughter. I am increasingly bewildered by her silence, and also by her stiff posture – almost as if she were playing the game 'Statues'. Embarrassingly, I begin to make pitiful interjections: 'That part about the twinkling eyes is really funny, isn't it?' Finally, realising I am flogging a dead horse, I also lapse into silence. I can't remember what she says when she finishes reading. I have already given this particular ploy away as a lost cause.

Susannah

Robin's campaign intensifies over the weeks, climaxing with her offering the phone to me while talking to Tim one evening. 'Do you want to say hello?' she mouths, bringing the phone yet closer to me. She is surprised I don't take up her offer. I am floored she made it.

But there is perhaps another, much bigger reason I am so reluctant to meet Tim: Dad.

I am terrified of telling Dad about any of this. At the beginning, I didn't think I had to: after all, I was only writing a better letter to my birth mother, resolving and finishing things. I didn't need to risk upsetting Dad over that. But now I am not finishing things, I am opening them right up and the fact that I haven't told Dad is starting to eat at me. I don't want to keep things from him but I fear his reaction: what if he thinks I am betraying him, and worse, betraying the memory of Mum? I worry that he will be hurt and then maybe angry, maybe so angry that he won't want to see me. That is too much to risk, so I don't say anything and I begin to fudge my replies when he asks what I've been up to, how things are. How things are? They are crazy: my son is on the final stretch of his VCE, still battling illness; my husband is building an exciting but challenging new business; and I am doing somersaults in my head as I try to work out my new reality. And I'm not telling my father.

Meanwhile, Robin continues her campaign of family integration and I wade in deeper and deeper with my blood family, increasingly feeling I am cheating on my life and love family.

My family and my biological friends

Susannah

Within my family, only Oskar and the kids know about my reunion with Robin. Oskar is completely supportive but increasingly alarmed at the speed and intensity of things, while Emma is enthusiastic and curious. Edvard is simply uninterested. 'If it makes you happy, Mum, that's great,' he says. 'But I don't want to meet them.'

And fair enough too. At eighteen, Edvard is more in the separating-from-family phase than seeking out more, and I have no desire to force anything on him. From time to time, he asks how things are with my 'biological friends', as he has named them, but he is never looking for a long answer and I never give him one.

Emma on the other hand wants to know all about them, what they look like, how they are, what they do – and whether she would see herself in any of them.

'I always hoped you would do this, Mum,' she says one day. 'I would never have told you but I'm happy you have.'

185

This surprises me and makes me happy – Robin isn't the only one who wants everyone to be together. Yet I am careful not to force anything on anyone. It has been a huge year for my family, yet soon both my children will head off to the other side of the world, Emma to spend a term at a Swedish school with her cousins and Edvard to a music course in London.

Poor Oskar, bless him, thought our six weeks of trial empty-nesting would be a couple's paradise – but he hadn't counted on the whirlwind of the biological dance, and he is already a little taken aback by the turn of events.

Oskar has suffered the most, really. There he was one moment with a stable, competent, if at times over-thinking wife who was just writing one letter to her birth mother – and then BAM! Competent, stable wife takes over-thinking to a new art form and spends most of her time either talking to said birth mother or talking about her. Meals are cooked, kids are wrangled and work is done, but his wife is consumed by this woman and these people who to him – and let's face it, to me – are complete strangers.

'It's like you've been kidnapped,' he says one evening after I get off the phone from another long call with Robin.

'No it's not!' I say, more than a little defensively.

'You're here but you're not,' he persists.

'No!' I protest. But he is right. And now with even more biologicals looming on the horizon, I know I am going to impose even more on my poor husband.

I think the solution might be for him to meet Robin, so he will become part of the whole thing, not just an increasingly alarmed observer. So, I suggest that he comes up to Longleaf and spends some time with Robin and me. Longleaf is one of Oskar's favourite places in the world, where he truly relaxes and where, I reason, he will be the most relaxed to meet the woman who has hijacked his wife's head and heart. And he can ride his motorbike up to join us, a long beautiful ride, filling him with calm and a love of life. It will be perfect, I think. I am wrong.

Robin and I arrive first, so when Oskar roars up the drive of Longleaf on his motorbike, we both come out to meet him. Robin looks a little nervous as Oskar, somewhat menacing in his leathers and black helmet, moves towards her saying, 'Hello, I'm Oskar.' 'Hello, Oskar,' she replies. 'I'm Robin.'

I note, a little worriedly, that neither hand nor hug is offered by either. *Oh well*, I think, *softly, softly*. Things will warm up.

And they do, but not in the way I hope for.

Unpacked and inside, Oskar seems displeased at things around the house; he identifies issues that are invisible to me yet, it seems, are my fault. He also seems oblivious to the fact we have a guest. It is excruciatingly embarrassing for me as I watch my husband lose it in front of Robin, minutes after meeting her.

'Why have you put the heater on?' he demands.

'Because it was a little cold,' I answer.

Grunt.

'Have you turned the watering system on?'

'No.'

Grunt.

'When,' he demands, holding a small tap nozzle, 'did this break?'

'I know!' I say. 'We only just got it. It came off yesterday, not sure how.'

Grunt. Grunt. Possibly a growl.

Let's be clear, this is not my husband stomping around our little weekender finding fault: this is some grumpy force on whom seemingly calming bike rides have no effect. I am unsure what to do to head him off, to calm him down. And then I see the cap-gun mini-explosives I bought thinking they might come in handy to distract or amuse a visiting child. They might work, the perfect distraction.

187

'Look!' I cry, possibly overenthusiastically. 'I bought these. I thought they might be fun.' And then Oskar literally goes ballistic and starts throwing the caps. At me.

This is too much. I need to get him out of here, away from Robin. What on earth must she be thinking? 'Oskar,' I say, ducking his last missile. 'There's something else broken outside.'

'What?!'

'Nothing too bad, just this thing,' I say, heading out the door, hoping I am luring him out too. 'Come and look. It's outside.'

'You've broken something else?' he growls, glowering as he stomps towards me, falling for my bait.

No, but I'm about to, I think as I go outside and head into the garden, Grumpy stomping behind me. When we are safely out of earshot of the house, it is my turn to unload.

'What do you think you're doing?' I ask.

Oskar looks stunned. 'What do you mean?'

I am stunned he looks stunned. 'Why are you finding fault with everything, with me, in front of Robin, minutes after meeting her? Why is that a good idea? And why were you throwing explosives at me?'

'They're not explosives, they're actually just caps …'

'Oskar!'

'Well, they're not – and what am I finding fault with?'

'Heater, watering, tap.'

'Ah,' his face softens a little. 'Well, maybe'.

'So, what are you doing?'

'I don't know, sorry.'

I think I do, though; by criticising me, Oskar is doing his impression of a caveman dragging his wife around by the hair in front of other, potentially threatening, cave people: *She is mine, I can do what I want to her, she's not yours. Deal with it.* But I didn't marry a caveman, I married a lovely and enlightened Swede whom I loved – and whom, it seems, I have now pushed to the limit.

I feel sorry for him, my poor neglected husband, and now it's my turn to soften.

'Oskar, do you think if we go back inside you can be more normal?'

'Nothing about this is normal, though, is it?' he says, and I sense his anger rising again.

'No,' I concede. 'But can we try anyway?'

'I am trying …'

'Not today you're not.'

'Okay, fair enough.'

I give my poor husband a hug. 'Well,' I offer, 'at least it's not me being mental for a change.'

Grunt. But it's a happier grunt this time and we head back to the house and Robin.

Robin

I have been looking forward to meeting Oskar but now I am a little startled by his behaviour. I sense he is not his normal self, but I feel for Susannah, for her humiliation in front of me. When they both return to the house, however, they appear to have sorted themselves out and the squall that engulfed Oskar has abated. He comes in smiling and sets about preparing drinks.

Susannah

Things improve (they could hardly get worse). Oskar plays host and Robin is brilliant at drawing him out about his work and his beloved 'Longie'. By the time we are sitting on the verandah watching the sun set magnificently behind Mount Alexander, there is even something approaching conviviality.

Robin

The next morning, Susannah and I take Oskar to the dam to view the water lilies she has purchased, inspired by a vision of a wonderland of floating colour. Although, looking at the rather sad, half-submerged plants it requires a lot of faith to believe in this vision, Oskar, in a generous attempt to atone for his sins of the previous day, overcorrects, and extols the lilies so hyperbolically that it is almost as disturbing as his fault-finding flurry had been.

I start to realise the conflicted feelings Oskar must have over Susannah's and my reunion and how threatening it is for him. Unfortunately, I am still not sufficiently sensitive to his feelings and I undoubtedly further spook the poor man by declaring, as I give him a farewell hug: 'There will be more!'

In retrospect, I see how ominous this must have sounded to someone already valiantly struggling to cope with the 'less'.

Balancing the biologicals

Susannah

By late spring I have met Matilda, her two gorgeous daughters
Ada and Aziza (how brilliant to have two daughters with palin-
drome names) and her soon-to-be husband Jason. It is undeniably
fun, but I am still trying to pace myself and my introduction
to Robin's – my? – family. Robin seems less interested in such
caution: she is now keen for me to meet her youngest daughter
Marian and, as I am learning, a keen Robin is a hard Robin to
say no to.

We are at a cafe over on her side of town one morning when
Robin receives a text message.

'Oh no! She's terrible!'

'Who is?' I ask.

'It's Marian,' she says. 'She wants to know where we're sitting.'

'She what?' I splutter.

'She says she's driving past the cafe and is trying to see us
but can't!'

I have to try very hard to overcome my impulse to dive under
the table. 'She's outside?' I ask. 'Here?'

'Yes! I did tell her what cafe we were meeting at and now it seems she's doing a bit of spying,' replies Robin. She seems to find this drive-by espionage amusing: I find it unnerving.

'I really want to meet Marian,' I start, 'but I need just a little bit of warning …'

'Yes, of course, Susannah,' replies Robin. 'It's fine.'

Hmmm fine. That word again

Ping! Robin receives another text.

'It's Marian again,' she says. 'She's given up and driven away.'

I relax but also realise that resistance is useless.

So, of course, when Marian and I do meet, it's only fitting that we return to the cafe of surveillance. Robin, Marian, her cherubic son Levi and I chat over coffee. Robin gently guides the conversation to start with but it soon gathers a momentum of its own. Marian is lovely – kind-hearted, quick-witted and funny – and, although held somewhat hostage to the will of a one-year-old who can't decide whether he wants to eat or wear his muffin, we talk easily. I recognise in Marian the same way with words that seems to make everyone in this family so easy to talk to, and to warm to. Immediately I know I like her and I want to know her better.

So, I have the idea that the four of us – Robin, Matilda, Marian and I – might all do something together before I leave to spend Christmas overseas. I offer a Christmas present of a relaxation massage for us all. If ever relaxation is a good idea, it is now, with this family. The idea is embraced and the next week we all enjoy a fun afternoon, first being gently pummelled by masseurs and then amusingly entertained by each other as we talk over coffee and cake. It is relaxed and easy and, driving home, I have a sense of contentment that has been eluding me recently.

It doesn't last long. I am home later than I said I would be and Oskar is, understandably, a bit put out. Luckily we are going out to dinner with friends and I hope that will diffuse the tension.

We arrive at the restaurant, order drinks and begin to update each other on our lives. The biological update is requested and given, although I try to be brief and breezy and give my husband a break.

'You're spending a lot of time with them, aren't you?' says one friend.

'Well, yes and there are a lot of them,' I say.

'A lot,' confirms Oskar.

'And you want to meet everyone?'

Oskar answers for me. 'She does.'

'Not all—' I start but don't get to finish.

'And if she isn't seeing them, she's talking to them or about them,' my husband adds.

'That's not true,' I protest.

'Isn't it?' asks Oskar.

It is a bit. 'Well, a little,' I concede. 'Shall we order?' Good try, Susannah.

'You won't forget about us, will you?' asks my friend.

'No! Of course not!'

'That's good. It does seem they have an express lane into your heart. We've been here for years.'

Oskar looks gratefully at my friend. I am a little shell-shocked. She says it beautifully, but a strong message is there: *We're not sure about these biological-come-latelys leapfrogging into the inner circle, that's our place. And we've been here the whole time. Don't forget us.*

And of course I won't, I can't. I haven't stopped loving the wonderful family and friends I already have but clearly they feel I am neglecting them. The adoption conversation that we have been having for decades is no longer hypothetical, it is now real and not everyone is as happy about it as I am. And if my friends are thinking this, what is the rest of my family feeling? Have I become so wrapped up in my 'new family' that I am, indeed, not looking after the 'old'?

Just as I realise I want to speed things up, to meet more of Robin's family, I get the message to slow down. But do I have to choose? Can't I have both? I'm not taking away, I'm just adding.

Aren't I?

Throwing the stone
into the pool

Robin

The addition of any new element to a situation, by definition, disturbs and changes the status quo. As a stone thrown into a pool displaces the water, causing droplets to sparkle and ripples to spread, messing with the general configuration, so the arrival of this new daughter into our family brings wonder and joy but also unsettling feelings of anxiety and potential threat as the other three wonder where their place might turn out to be once the whirlpool stops whirling. Is more always more, or can it be less?

Anna, Matilda and Marian welcome and delight in the discovery of their new-found sister. The signs of the shared gene pool – especially with Anna and Matilda, Tim's daughters – are fascinating to observe: not only physical resemblances, but also ways of talking and laughing that are uncannily similar.

However, every now and then, thrown up by emotional churnings below, fears and doubts break through the surface like little jumping fish: 'You will like her more than me because she is more talented and successful than I am' … 'You are more affectionate to her than you have ever been to me – you never hold my hand' … 'She's had her mother, why should she come and take ours?'

The ripple effect also spreads to their relationships with each other, reflecting pre-Susannah insecurities – 'She clicks more with her than with me,' or 'I feel left out.'

This in turn triggers wrong responses from me, causing me to fall into the old 'fixer' trap, taking false and inappropriate responsibility. I step into the role of go-between, trying to negate their fears ('No, I'm sure that's not true …') and to manipulate the situation by suggestions ('Perhaps you could give her a call … she said she hadn't heard back from you; did you answer her last text? I think it would be nice to include her in that …').

While attempting to be a peacemaker, I too often become a managing middle-man – getting myself into trouble and making things worse all round. If there is anything at all to be learned from watching *The Bold and the Beautiful* it is surely the havoc caused by too much intervention in the affairs of others.

So – the introduction of Susannah into the mix has really stirred the pot! For good or for bad? Is it a wrecking ball or a blessing bomb? It is sometimes difficult to tell the difference; renovation nearly always entails some demolition. I personally have no doubt that her return to us is a blessing – part of God's plan of healing and restoration for the whole family.

Pressing pause

Susannah

Things are all getting a bit much on both sides of the family fence as both Robin and I wrangle our tribes and each other.

Yet now, in early December, I am about to step off the wonderful but giddying carousel by travelling overseas with Oskar to reclaim our children, see my brother and his family in Cambridge and then celebrate Christmas with our family in Sweden. We have planned to bid farewell to 2014 and start what we hope will be a calmer 2015 at the very top of the world in the Arctic Circle. The four of us reunited in a glass igloo in the middle of a Finnish forest, hunting the northern lights on huskies and skidoos. I also think the break will be good for Robin and me: she has a lot going on in her family too, so this could be the perfect moment to press pause.

The adult me thinks this is a brilliant idea and the mother in me is beside myself with excitement at seeing Edvard and Emma again: both kids leaving the nest to go so far away has pulled hard on the phantom umbilical cord and I can't wait to see them both.

But that pesky inner child, however, is also beside herself and doesn't want to go so far away for so long. It is a weird tug of war that perhaps I should have seen coming, but I didn't.

The night before Oskar and I fly out, Robin and I go out for dinner. The restaurant is delightful on a warm summer evening and the food is delicious, but I am already beginning to worry about leaving. It doesn't help that I am also an anxious flyer and the anticipation of the long flight is adding to my stress. I try not to show any of this to Robin as we make our way through the ridiculous amount of food that we have, in our enthusiasm, over-ordered. We then go back to Robin's house and watch a DVD, a good distraction. Yet as the movie comes to an end, so too, I realise, has my time with Robin. I am excited about our trip but, right now, I don't want to leave.

Robin

I can't let my daughter go all that distance away without praying for her. I ask the Lord to watch over her and keep her and her family safe. I pray that their time together will be bonding and that their Christmas will be full of peace and jollity.

Susannah

I understand that the prayer is important for Robin and I am comforted by her words and her hug but it isn't enough: I want something more tangible that I can take with me, have with me while we are apart. Robin takes a green cord from some flowers I have given her and cuts it: we tie one part around my wrist and another on her key-ring. Tethered. That is the theory. The string will hold tight, the knot cannot be loosened. It is a symbol of our unbreakable connection.

The symbol crashes and burns within the hour.

I haven't even left Hadfield when I look at my wrist and the ribbon isn't there. I U-turn back to Robin's house. She tries to make a joke of it but I will have none of it, so she runs back inside and finds more cord. This time she ties it tighter with a complicated but ineffectual series of knots. When I get home, Oskar, sensing his wife is, once again, close to losing it, burns the ends to hold it fast. That cord isn't going anywhere.

But I am, and it is with a strange mixture of excitement and regret that I board the plane to Europe towards my family and 17 000 miles away from Robin.

Family reunion

Susannah

Oskar and I have an idyllic stopover in Dubai before we land in London. Two days of sun and sleep are just what is needed before we fly on to stay with much-loved old friends and to be reunited with Edvard, who has in turn just been reunited with his girlfriend, Claudia. And then, reunions clearly the order of the day, we all travel to Cambridge and reunite with my brother Duncan and his family, and Dad, who is staying with them.

Cambridge is a charming university city and Duncan, a fellow at one of the colleges, has arranged a beautiful dinner in a private dining room at St John's. It is very Cambridge yet also very family, with old jokes being told and a lifetime of shared experiences and anecdotes being drawn on and traded. Everyone knows their role; there is no wondering if you have put your foot in something, made a good or bad impression. Everyone just is as they have always been and it is so easy, relaxed and lovely.

I watch my dad, my brother and my nephew together – three peas in a genetic pod – and with fresh eyes I see the strength of their similarities, both in appearance and manner, the expressions they use, even the looks they give. And, as I watch my niece, I can see both her mum and my mum in her. The similarities are as undeniable as they are comforting.

I don't remember it ever worrying me that I couldn't see myself in anyone else in my family, but I realise that I like that I can now: that I can hear my laugh in Matilda's, that I can see my jaw-line in Robin's. It isn't essential but, then again, there is something affirming about it.

For a moment I have a thought that this might be the time to tell my family about my other family. The atmosphere is so warm and loving … and I want to throw a hand grenade at it? So I keep that thought to myself but with a little sadness: once again I am hiding something important from the people I love.

But this is not the time for sadness: there is too much fun to be had. We return to London: we shop among the Christmas lights of Regent Street, see a brilliant play in the West End and we eat and drink our way through the week with festive cheer and abandon.

Yet, every now and then, I feel a pang. I miss Robin. I am surrounded by family and old friends and the excitement of being in London at Christmas time, yet part of me wants to be back in Hadfield. What is that about?

Oskar suggests that I ring Robin, to keep up a bit of contact, and keep me in check. 'Just don't talk too long,' Oskar wisely advises. 'We are still on Australian SIM cards and it will cost a fortune.'

I ring Robin late one night, which is early in the morning for her. Things are difficult for her at home, she is tired and I am jetlagged and we have a small argument over nothing. An hour later, things aren't much better – I can't believe I am paying this much to become this upset. I hang up, sad, and then get a text from Robin. She is, inexplicably to me, excited:

Our first argument! Great! Sign of intimacy xx

Now I am even sadder. Not only am I sad we argued when I really just wanted to be comforted by Robin's voice, but now she is claiming the argument is a good thing, a happy new stage in our relationship. And Oskar is rightly wondering about our phone bill. None of this helps.

What does help, however, is flying to Sweden towards one last reunion, with Emma, and a Christmas with Oskar's family. Sweden and our Swedish family are very important to us and to be all together for Christmas, the first without Oskar and his sister Stina's mum, is particularly special. And the Swedes really know how to do Christmas: their response to the cold and dark of a Nordic winter is to make the preparations and lead-up to Christmas so beautiful that we all forget we are freezing in the dark.

And so it is as we enter Stina and Sten's house, one of my favourite places in the world, now exquisitely decorated with candles, handcrafted paper stars in the hallway and a magnificent Christmas tree in the corner of the living room. The smell of the Christmas fir, the gingerbread cookies and blue cheese and the bottle of chilled wine greet us in the living room. My daughter arrives home from a party and the family is all together again. I watch my two children sit so happily with their cousins, this time five peas in a genetic pod, and there is a lovely sense of calm and belonging. I feel incredibly lucky.

VIII

EMOTION SICKNESS

Buffeted by the waves

Robin

I have severe igloo envy. The idea of quiet, remote isolation seems incredibly appealing to me, as back in the heat of the Australian summer, the pressure is on: there is Matilda's wedding to Jason to organise and other serious family issues erupt just before Christmas.

On top of all this, probably as a result of lifting my grandson Levi incorrectly, I manage to injure a spinal disc, which then causes pressure on the sciatic nerve in my leg. As anyone who has experienced this will testify, it can be excruciatingly painful. I cannot afford to rest properly, however, because there is too much to do, but, when out and about, I am frequently reduced to taking emergency measures, such as walking bent over at a ninety-degree angle or sitting down on a stack of toilet rolls in Coles.

As an unattractive garnish to this mix of minor adversities, I have an accident that could have proved to be quite disastrous. I am sitting in a cane chair on Marian's outside deck, from which a flight of four stairs descends to the lawn, when a slight movement causes one leg of the chair to tip over the edge and I find myself, still in my cane chair, tumbling backwards, over and over till

I land on the ground. Thank God, I emerge from the experience virtually unscathed. However, as a result of accumulated pressures, I am becoming increasingly physically and emotionally exhausted. I hope Susannah is having more of a refreshing break. I do miss her but maybe it's for the best that she is not here right now, given the tensions and busyness.

Separation anxiety in the snow

Susannah

With snow falling gently outside, there is, blissfully, no need for excuses to do nothing. The family takes long, rugged-up walks along a frozen beach and sits by the fire watching movies, reading books, talking, being together. And yet, I feel a little apart, adrift. Early on an already dark afternoon, my reading of choice is a raft of e-books about adoption, all with titles that involve colons, never the indicator of a light read. Yet I am hoping to learn, looking for knowledge that will give me some context and perspective on my reunion with Robin, some relief from the rising panic I am feeling.

All the books talk about how adoptees carry a deep, primal wound of abandonment and that, reunion or no reunion, they need to bring together a divided self that was split between their blood and life families. They describe the experience of the adoptee attempting reunion as a bombardment of overpowering emotions that seems to come from nowhere and tosses them in all directions.

Six months ago I would have scoffed at all this but now I understand the motion sickness they describe, the lurching, heart in stomach, from one confused feeling to another. It is as if all the books are talking about me and my experience with Robin, looking into my heart and head. I love reading it: it shows that it isn't just me, that I'm not going mad – or if I am, it's okay, it's normal, it's to be expected. I realise with relief that if I am the nutter I fear I am, I am in the very good company of a large number of adoptees struggling to cope with a reunion.

And, as I read on, I discover that it is very common for adoptees to spend years denying the importance of their birth families. 'Hostile non-searchers', they, we, deny that any wound has been inflicted, that any connection to their birth families exists. Then, whenever, however that wound is exposed, everything is thrown up in the air: the genetic genie is out of the bottle and there's no turning back to the comfort of numb denial.

I read case study after case study and similar stories of alienated confusion and tumult are told. In my mind, I build an image of the adoptee straddling two countries, the one of their birth and the one of their life: they have a passport to both but perhaps never feel completely at home in either, walking a tightrope between the two.

I read on, flicking from book to book, Googling other references, and begin to build a list of my 'symptoms':

- Fear of telling my adoptive parents – tick, got that one covered.
- Trouble bringing the 'what was', the 'what ifs' and 'what is' together – tick, massive head spin.
- Trying to please everyone, fear of being abandoned all over again – tick.
- And then – separation anxiety if away from the birth mother once reunited.

Ah, there it is, the reason I feel like I did when leaving Robin to come overseas, the reason I am still feeling sad when I am surrounded by everyone I love. My inner child has popped up again and now has a severe case of separation anxiety. But what can I do about it?

'Time for wine, Suse?'

My darling sister-in-law offers me a glass and I put down my iPad.

'What are you reading?'

'Nothing much.'

I told Stina about Robin and the reunion soon after we arrived in Sweden but I don't want to discuss this. This information is all new and I need to wrestle it by myself a bit.

And we have Christmas to plan. There is a long list of decisions to be made about what will be cooked and when and by whom to prepare the *julbord*, the Swedish Christmas table. The kids are allocated the meatball-making, Sten will prepare his Danish dishes, and Stina and I will do the gravlax. There is a lot to plan and much shopping to be done but it is far from a chore: it's part of Christmas and it's fun and it's very family. Stina and I have both done it with Stina's mum before and now we are doing it without her but together: the family renews and reknits. Stina and I talk easily and with love: despite no blood bond and only seeing each other every two years, there is a deep, mutual tie. Family comes in all different boxes.

Later that night, while everyone sleeps, my mind spins again and I return to my books. As I read, it seems the adoptee's separation anxiety is best healed if the birth mother is prepared to acknowledge it, to see the wounded baby in the adult child and help it to heal.

Part of me, instinctively, cries out *yes please* and that's what I asked for and she gave me at Longleaf. But can I keep asking her and for how long? I don't want this to go on forever either – I would quite like my grown-up self back in charge. I Google on, looking for answers and I find myself once again watching Professor Brené Brown's brilliant TED talk on vulnerability. She speaks of the need to be brave enough to show up as we really are, to allow ourselves to be seen, to reveal ourselves to others as vulnerable and, above all else, to believe ourselves to be worthy of love and ask for it.

Big call for the baby abandoned. But perhaps I can lay a path. I take a screen shot of a page from one of the books about re-parenting the reunited adult child and send it to Robin. And I hope it doesn't freak her out completely.

Robin

I am a little horrified by the whole re-parenting thing. Being a single mother, especially with both myself and my children bearing wounds from the past, wasn't easy. I carried burdens that I should have cast on the Lord as He tells us to do, and in hanging on to them, I think I often messed up His operations and depleted my resources. As a hangover from this, when I read in the adoption literature Susannah sends that the adoptee can need considerable re-parenting, I must admit I quail at the thought. Who has a baby at seventy-two? One phrase used by a psychologist was 'sucking on the withered breast', which epitomises the taxing and at times despairing feeling of not being able to give what is demanded. 'Give more! Feel more! Do more!' Blood out of a stone.

Sometimes, in rebellion against the tossing of the waves, *my* inner child rises up: *Poor me. It's too hard! It's not fair!*

But then I remind myself that I can go to Jesus, who is my harbour of rest and, no matter how rough the seas, He is the anchor that holds me fast, that tethers and calms my soul. He is the navigator I am relying on in this voyage with Susannah and because I believe He is in our little boat with us, I believe we will make it safely home.

So, I rally and send Susannah this email:

Hello darling.

I have only now discovered this email as I haven't 'gone on the computer' for some time. It is very interesting and validates any 'nuttiness' you may have manifested, as it seems clear that being adopted ranks very high on the trauma scale. I don't think this is at all widely appreciated – and certainly not by me.

One tends to think of other things – like witnessing horrors as a child or being abused as a child or even later being abandoned as a child, for example, would be worse than 'being given away to a better family' at birth.

The whole identity issue – and the fact that this begins before emerging at birth even – is little understood and therefore little taken in to account – but is, in fact, obviously crucial! Again, good old Shakespeare comes to mind: 'there are more things in heaven and earth than are dreamt of in our philosophy'. So, darling Susannah, I am more conscious now of the magnitude of the 'sin' (my term for the wrongness of our ways) in giving you away – in ignorance, maybe, but ignorance doesn't mitigate consequences). In your early letter, all those years ago, you said – also out of ignorance – you had nothing to forgive me for. Thank you for recently – with more understanding – telling me that you did forgive me; that was a beautiful thing.

Looking forward to having you back here.

All my love, Robin xx

Susannah

Robin's email makes me happy: she seems to understand that I am more comfortable with her invoking Shakespeare than the Bible. The differences between Robin and me are becoming clearer at the same time as the strength of the connection is being confirmed. It's more than a little confusing.

So, I ponder my newly diagnosed separation anxiety and decide I need to do something about it. Perhaps I need distractions from Robin, things to help me wean myself from her? And then it comes to me, the perfect solution – I'll make contact with Tim.

Up until now I have been a conscientious objector to meeting Tim, largely because I don't know what to do with him – and don't know what he would do with me. Robin has assured me that he wants to meet me but part of me thought, why would he really? He hasn't ever before.

But 17 000 miles away it suddenly seems a brilliant idea. So, I ask Robin for his number. She sounds surprised.

Robin

Despite the fact that I have been so keen for Tim and Susannah to connect, I am surprised that she should choose this time to make contact. Somehow it seems a little impetuous, a little crazy. I feel she should stop spinning, stop throwing more and more balls into the air – slow down her already frenetic juggling of people, thoughts, emotions. Why doesn't she take this holiday opportunity to rest and regroup? I am exhausted just thinking about her energy! But then maybe that's the tortoise in me coming out: older, slower, increasingly averse to doing more than one thing at a time.

I give the hare Tim's number.

Susannah

Robin seems reluctant to give me the number. Now it's my turn to press. She concedes and I send Tim a text. I'm more than a little chuffed when he replies, saying he is delighted to be in contact. Apparently not a man for texting, he asks for my email address, and an amusing if careful exchange of emails ensues. Before I know it, we seem to have agreed on a day and a place to have lunch in Melbourne on my return. And far away in Sweden, that seems a brilliant idea too.

Family Christmases

Susannah

On Christmas morning, the whole family walks through the forest to a small, whitewashed sixteenth-century church that perches on the coast, outside the town. We visit my mother-in-law's burial place. As was her wish, there is no stone but she is buried in a shared plot overlooking the beach she used to love to walk on. No one talks much: everyone has their memories of Mamma, Bette, Farmor and, together, we each remember.

We return home and the Christmas table is set, first with the hand-embroidered cloth that Bette made and then the special dinner plates and glasses. Candles are lit throughout the house, meatballs are warmed, herring after herring dish is laid out and, as the Christmas smorgasbord builds, so too does the sense of celebration. Once all is ready, everyone goes to change into their Christmas best ready for champagne and oysters. Sten's sister and husband arrive: more family into the fold.

God Jul! Merry Christmas!

We drink, we eat, we laugh, we talk, we eat. Living so far away from each other, we all know how few Christmases we spend together and everyone embraces the time. There are speeches and songs, as there must be in Sweden, and when everyone can eat no more we move into the living room and sit around the Christmas tree for presents. The teenagers become children again as they wait for their gifts and somehow yet more food is eaten. Hearts and stomachs are very, very full.

I send a text to Robin wishing them all a very happy Christmas.

Robin

The Christmas scene back here in Oz couldn't be more different than that in Sweden. Given that Matilda's wedding to Jason is to take place on 3 January, our celebration this year is more low key.

We have customarily celebrated the feast along the lines of the English model – roast turkey with all the trimmings, plum pudding implanted with tiny treasures and accompanied by cream, ice-cream and brandy sauce – but this year we go for the informal barbie. The venue is Susan's very large back garden and the scene is quintessentially Australian.

I love it. The weather is perfect and a summer heat haze shimmers over the wide lawn. The table is laid in the green mansion of the huge peppercorn tree and I can't resist breaking off a small sprig to crush in my fingers, releasing the deliciously spicy smell of the leaves and berries. Lounging back in my chair, I idly watch the menfolk in aprons, beers in hand, tending the meat on the barbecue. I'm glad not to be cooking this year.

It is wonderful to have Anna and her family back from Vanuatu, and home to stay this time. Jason's son, Jake, has come over from America for the wedding, so he is also with us. A spreading family – my vision again – and now including Susannah, my reclaimed first daughter, and her family. A Bible verse comes to me (as they tend to do): 'In my Father's house are many mansions'. Room for everyone. Welcome one and all.

Susannah

On New Year's Eve my little family of four is in an igloo deep in the Arctic Circle. Watching for northern lights that never come, it is still entrancing to be in this snow-covered forest. It's almost impossible not to think back over the year and look to the year ahead, and my thoughts inevitably turn to family. These three precious people standing in the cold preparing to watch the midnight fireworks are my family. Duncan in Cambridge is family, Dad and Sophie back home are family and the Sörensens in Sweden are family. And now I have more family. The concept is as small or as expandable as you and your heart want to make it. Standing in pristine snow at the top of world everything seems very simple, uncomplicated. I resolve to not get so worked up about things when I get home and to try to just enjoy all these lovely people in my life, regardless of where they fit and how long they have been there.

But, as we all know, New Year's resolutions aren't always so easy to keep.

Back together – and falling apart?

Susannah

We arrive back home and I am really looking forward to seeing Robin again but it seems almost impossible to find a day when she is available. My excitement, mixed with jetlag, soon moves to a deflated disappointment. In the end I have to settle for joining her while she babysits Levi, who today seems to have the edge on me in maturity.

I feel like I have been fitted in. When we meet, while she seems pleased to see me, I don't get much of a hug. She seems happy enough with my gifts but it feels like she hasn't really missed me that much – and once again I feel like the needy one in a much-too-lopsided relationship. So, I decide it was a mistake to come: I should have waited for a day when I could have her undivided attention. At least now, thanks to my holiday reading, I am beginning to understand what might be going on in my messed-up, regressed mind even if I can't always control the reaction.

So, I decide to leave rather than hang around waiting for scraps of attention. I say I need to go and Robin, understandably preoccupied with her very mobile grandson, says goodbye. I give her a rushed kiss and leave – I cannot get out of there quickly enough.

Robin

It was lovely to see Susannah again; I am very glad she is back and am looking forward to having proper undistracted time with her on Thursday. I may be imagining it, but she seemed a little strange with me. I have the vague feeling I have done something wrong, but I don't know what. Perhaps she thinks I didn't focus on her enough after her absence, but I just couldn't with Levi demanding my attention.

Maybe I should text her.

Sorry it was so busy today. We will have our time together soon.

Susannah

I ignore Robin's text. I cannot believe this is happening again, that I am going nutty, feeling unsettled again; what a blow for my igloo resolutions of calm, and so soon.

So, I message my third sister Anna, now returned from Vanuatu, and we arrange to meet over dinner. Perhaps, as with Tim, another biological friend will provide some distraction from Robin and the intensity of our reunion.

Throwing an Anna
in the works

Susannah

Anna and I have agreed to meet at a restaurant halfway between our two homes. I arrive first and she soon after. We give each other a tentative hug and sit down.

'Drink?' I ask.

'Just the one,' says Anna. 'I've got the car.'

'Oh,' I say. I have to say that I'm a little gutted. I admit I was hoping that we would make a night of it and while I know alcohol is not essential to that, driving does seem un-encouragingly cautious of Anna. She must sense (she will later claim that she is psychic when it comes to me) my disappointment.

'Didn't you drive?' she asks.

'No, taxi.'

'Oh.'

'Oh well, not to worry,' I rally as I pretend. 'It's not a problem.'

Drinks are ordered and the conversation starts, politely to begin with, about each other's work and our kids, but it soon dives deeper and we talk about everything – the reunion and the weirdness, her childhood, my childhood, Robin, my mum; no area seems off limits and we are both completely relaxed with that. It is also clear that a short dinner and two drinks will not be long enough, so we concoct a cunning plan.

We drop Anna's car back at her apartment and plot our next move in an unremarkable wine bar nearby. There's nothing wrong with the bar, it's completely fine, but we are both feeling we need something so much more than fine.

'We could,' I suggest, 'go to my favourite place in Melbourne, possibly the world.'

'Where?' asks Anna, clearly up for it.

'It's called Siglo,' I said. 'It's this really beautiful rooftop—'

'I know!' breaks in Anna. 'That's *my* favourite place!'

Of course it is, it makes complete sense and we gleefully leap into a taxi and head off into the city and to our favourite place.

We laugh a lot and cry easily, often at the same time and, without thinking, touch each other's arm or take a hand in moments of intensity or hilarity – it is strangely and strongly familiar and I feel, I know, I've just met a new best friend. No, scratch that, a sister.

Ten hours later we both decide it's probably time to go home and, at 4am, we have no problem getting a taxi. Anna sends me a text while I am still in the taxi.

That was wonderful. I am so happy to have you in my life xxx

The feeling is completely mutual.

So happy, in fact, that I feel that Anna needs to be shared immediately with my family, so I suggest to Oskar that she, her husband, Dominique, and their two young sons, Matthieu and Theo, come for a casual dinner at our place on the Friday. I think it's a brilliant idea.

'Yes!' says Emma.

'This Friday?' asks Oskar.

'Yes,' I confirm. 'You will really like Anna.'

'This Friday before we go to Matilda and Jason's gig on the Sunday and before you meet Tim on the Monday?'

'Yes,' I say, slightly less confidently. 'But you're just doing two of them,' I venture.

'You don't think that's overdoing it, even for you?' ventures my husband.

It had never crossed my mind. It does now, briefly, but then flies out again.

'Well, might as well make it a festival,' he says with only the smallest of sighs.

'Exactly!' I cry, exultant, and with what I hope is a very grateful look at my biologically bombarded husband. 'It will be fun! I promise.'

And my promise is easily kept. The initial mutual shyness at the front door between children and adults alike lasts approximately ten minutes, blasted out by the warmth and desire to connect and enjoy. Emma, normally reserved when meeting new people, especially adults, embraces the conversation. Anna declares that she and I are identical. She genuinely believes this and is utterly immune to any argument to the contrary: that her hair is dark brown and mine is fair (neither, I hasten to point out, naturally anymore) and that her eyes are brown and mine are blue are, apparently, technicalities of interest only to the pedant. Anna loves that we are identical: I love that she loves it, however deluded that may be.

Emma is not completely convinced and begins questioning her newly acquired aunt on the issue. The ensuing verbal joust delights them both – and me, who can't resist joining in. Oskar and Dominique stand back in amused amazement and then Theo, Anna and Dominique's four-year-old, climbs on to Emma's lap and stays there.

Sometimes four-year-olds just cut through stuff.

Lying in bed later that night, I realise that there isn't and doesn't have to be anything complicated about Anna and me. We just get each other, without having to try. And while we both seem to carry the needy good-girl desire-to-please gene we don't have to try with each other – we just make each other happy.

Am I finally getting the hang of this biological-friend thing?

Meeting Tim

Susannah

Two days later and after a sleepless night I call Robin on the morning I am due to meet with Tim. I seem to have lost my biological-friend bravado.

'Robin, will you be disappointed if I don't go to lunch?'

'What? Why don't you want to go to lunch?'

'I don't think I can.'

'Why not?'

'I won't know what to do.'

'Let him do it.'

'But you won't be angry if I don't go?'

'No, of course not, darling!'

Sorted. But then I picture an elderly man sitting alone in the restaurant and realise that, of course, I have to go – it's too rude and too unfair to bail at the last moment.

So, we head off. Oskar drives me and we do blocks around St Kilda until it's ten minutes after one o'clock. I don't want to be the first one there: I have completely over-analysed it and decided that that would appear too needy. No, he definitely needs to be the one to arrive first.

Tim

Charmayne drops me off at the bottom of Fitzroy Street, after a kerfuffle concerning wrong turns down Beaconsfield Parade and a U-turn into a 96 tram brought on by my inner tension, not unlike that before attending auditions or a blind date.

So, I get out on the wrong side of the road and jaywalk into the traffic over to where I know for sure Di Stasio is. It isn't. I walk back a bit till I think that no way is it this far up, and then I walk down again until finally, right outside Di Stasio, I desperately ask a passer-by where it is.

After only a minor contretemps with the door as I step into the posh, poky, crepuscular L-shaped joint, I am sat down at a lamplit little table for two with a view of the entrance, the first to arrive, reluctantly refusing a drink, or perhaps not, and trying to collect myself.

I have decided to dress Somerset Maughamy. Graham Greenish, a touch of the Old South from where we share a gene pool. Cool, gravitas. I have brought along some photos of my mother. I drop them on the floor. Gathering them up I notice a stain on an inside sleeve of my beige, Maughamy–Greenish jacket. Largish. Cacky, some copious regurgitation from a feeding parrot, dried stiff. The occasion is taking a Kingsley Amis direction.

I may well have called for chardonnay at this point.

Susannah

I walk into the restaurant and croak out my name to the waiter.

'Oh yes,' a croakless waiter replies. 'A gentleman is waiting here for you. This way, please.'

I swallow. *Okay, this is it*, I think. *Let's do this.*

As the waiter brings me into the restaurant my eyes dart and then lock on an elderly not-un-Santa-like man with a white beard, who is rising from a table and looking at me with a sort of smile. I hope I smile back as I approach him.

I put out my arms and nervously offer a hug.

'Hello.'

'Hello, Susannah.'

We hug a little awkwardly and then sit down. We look at each other, perhaps both relieved that we have both shown up, that the first hurdle is over. The waiter returns.

'Will you be having wine with lunch today?'

Oh yes bloody please and really quickly, I think but manage to ask for the wine list sounding, I hope, a little less desperate.

'Would you like a glass of wine, Tim?' I ask.

He doesn't need time to consider. We order a bottle.

Now what do we say? Tim apologises for what he thinks might be a bloodstain on his jacket. I say I hadn't noticed it – which I hadn't – and ask him how his appointment was. It was with a heart specialist, which strikes me as slightly ironic. All went well, so I hope that's an omen for the lunch.

Tim then offers me a copy of a book he's written, a history of the Pram Factory, a Melbourne theatre collective in the 1960s and 1970s. I am touched. I open it and see it is inscribed. I am about to be touched again when I see it is actually inscribed to someone else. I look a little quizzically up at Tim.

'Yes, feel a bit of an idiot, I didn't notice that when I picked it up. I'll take it back and give you another one.'

'No, don't worry,' I say. 'Perhaps we can adjust the inscription?'

It is Tim's turn to look quizzical.

I take out my pen. 'Well, we could convert it, draw over it?'

Tim seems game but then I remember that I have absolutely no artistic ability whatsoever and, while I didn't suggest the activity as a platform for showing off to Tim, nor did I mean to create one to expose just how deeply bad I am at something.

'Um, I can't actually draw but perhaps we could just draw over the "Merry Christmas Penny" part with some flowers or something.'

What am I saying?

'Okay,' he says, slightly unconvinced.

I start to 'draw' and Tim looks even less convinced. Perhaps he thinks I am now just defacing his book?

Wine arrives, thankfully, and with a gulp I continue scrawling over the original message with stem-like lines atop of which I draw flower petals: I am going for whimsical sketchy but it is just coming off messy scribble. Tim now has a bemused or possibly amused look on his face. I draw a square and write inside it: 'Tim's bit here.'

'Off you go,' I say, offering him my pen.

Tim draws something, a kind of beast moving into a slightly Picasso-esque female form and writes a speech bubble: 'Who are we?'

I am out of my depth. I panic, take another sip (gulp) of wine and respond by drawing one of the three things I have ever drawn with any confidence – a cartoon of a bearded man with glasses wearing an academic mortar board. It looks like my father, circa 1980s, when he received his Masters degree; that, along with a be-hatted penguin and a packet of McDonald's fries, are my go-to drawing set pieces. I think I should have gone the penguin, but the appalling drawing does lead to a conversation about fathers.

'I never thought fathers mattered as much,' offers Tim. 'More the mothers.'

'Well, you wouldn't, would you?' I reply gently, knowing from Robin that Tim never met his father. 'But I think they do. All types.'

And with that we continue to draw – well, one of us does – until our meals arrive.

Finally Tim signs the book: 'To my long-lost, new-found daughter Susannah, love Tim?'

I don't understand the question mark – does Tim not know who he is?

And then he shows me a photo of his mother, Janet.

'You look exactly like her,' he says.

I am a little taken aback: he thinks I look exactly like a 75-year-old woman?

I leave it, though, and we enjoy the meal and each other's conversation. It's so much easier than I thought it would be. It's actually fun and around the two-hour mark, Tim asks, 'Should Anna join us?'

I'm a little surprised but think, why not? 'But where is she?'

'Just around the corner,' he replies, looking a little sheepish.

'Really? Why?'

Tim comes clean: he had asked Anna to be close by in case the whole lunch was a disaster and he needed to be evacuated.

'And you don't need to be evacuated now?' I ask.

'No, not at all, this is wonderful! But Anna should join us too.'

And so Anna joins us and it is even more wonderful. She helps us finish our cheese and then we move to the bar where about an hour later Tim has another idea.

'Should Charmayne, Finn and Billie join us?'

Charmayne is Tim's wife and their children, Finn and Billie, are my half-brother and sister. I didn't realise they were close by.

'Why, are they around the corner too?' I ask. How many evac teams does one birth father need? I hesitate a little, though – that would be meeting four biologicals in a day, well over my quota. But Anna is with me and, strangely, this makes me feel close to bullet-proof. I make her promise she will stay and she immediately agrees.

'Why not, then?' I say to Tim. 'The more the merrier.'

And so, now we move to the tables outside and the sunshine. The go-slow on meeting the biologicals has gone completely out the window but it doesn't matter. Finn and Billie, much younger than me, look both disconcertingly and comfortingly like only slightly older versions of my children, and that weird familiarity seems to lubricate the conversation, of which there is much, hectic and hilarious. Indeed, everything conspires to make the lunch that turns into dinner a stunning success.

At one point, Tim just pats my hand and smiles, a broad, very happy smile. After eight hours of so many words, none are needed. We have both done well.

At 7pm I receive a text from Robin:

How was the lunch? X

I text back:

Still there – and Anna, Charmayne, Finn and Billie are here now too. It's lovely!

Robin replies:

Gosh!

As the sun sets into the St Kilda bay, we order more drinks to toast the lunch that nearly wasn't.

The next day I remember that I promised to send Tim my 'Heartbeat' poem. I'm a little nervous – no, actually, I'm very nervous – but I write a quick message, attach the poem, press send, and run away from my desk.

A couple of hours later this drops in to my inbox:

> *Your self-song my heart harrows:*
> *I hear the Babe Joan solo screaming*
> *Left unsuckled abandoned angry,*
> *mummadadda bailing after the biological bit,*
> *gone for good that's what they said.*
> *Forgive us we knew not what we …*
> *No end of forgetting and begetting*
> *life still hums love's loopy song*
> *makes you a heartmending mother*
> *delivers you an enduring dad*
> *Thank you Susannah for your lifelines*
> *the horror and happy harvest they bring home,*

and all your makings good
be kind to these awkward alliterates of mine
Love
Tim
X

And so begins a happy exchange of emails. Dictionary and Google by my side to look up the ever-obscure references and word-slams Tim creates; it is uncomplicated and joyful.

And I realise gratefully that both my fathers have given me the incredible gift of the love of language.

Down the 'what if' rabbit hole

Susannah

Meeting and roistering with the biologicals has been more than I – and even Robin – could have hoped for. It has been fun beyond measure but it has also had an unsettling effect on me.

Because the more time I spend with them, the more clicks we make, the more family photos I see and family anecdotes I hear, I can't help but wonder what it would have been like to have grown up with them all, how it would have been if Robin and Tim had kept me. I know it would have been a lot more turbulent than my childhood was and I am overwhelmingly grateful to Mum and Dad for the stable, calm – but also fun and adventure-filled – home, but there is also a pang of the what-if and it sends me down a rabbit hole of what-ifs that completely does my head in.

Essentially, if you think about it long enough you make so many people you love not exist – it's not a game I recommend playing.

It starts like this. I imagine that Robin did keep me and instantly there is no more Mum and Dad, no Duncan and Sophie, at least not for me. Someone else would have taken my place at Hawthorn Grove, my spot at school and at college. It is highly unlikely that I would have met Oskar and so there go Edvard and Emma, completely. They never exist, they are nothing more than an improbable genetic possibility that never gets realised. Now, that is an unbearable thought.

And then I get to work on Robin's family. Robin does keep me. What happens to Robin and Tim? A little unwanted baby is too much and they split earlier and all of a sudden – BAM! – no Anna, no Matilda. And with no them, none of their precious family exist either, and so it goes on. The reversal of one decision would have changed everything from the everything we know now to something else we can't imagine. It's like everyone in both families are just bubbles and one twist in events and POP! They're gone, erased, never to exist.

And I certainly don't want that. I don't wish any part of my life undone and replaced with something else. While I now mourn the loss I suffered as a baby, I don't regret being adopted by Mum and Dad. I absolutely don't regret the wonderful life I've had with them, but still I feel the pull of the divided self the adoption books describe and I feel rushes of sadness, anger in among the relief and gratitude. Bottom line, I want both: I don't wish what I had away but I wish I'd had more time with this family that looks and sounds like me.

It's like coming to a dinner party of really good friends – where everyone feels a click of comfort and ease with everybody else – except I have the time wrong and come late. By the time I arrive, the drinks, first and main courses have all been served and eaten, and some pretty meaty arguments and conversations have taken place. Most people are a little drunk, some very. And in I come, stone cold sober and with no idea of what I've missed.

They all look a little worse for wear but they're incredibly welcoming, almost ridiculously pleased to see me and I like them a lot. I try to catch up: I drink quickly, move around the table, smiling, talking to everybody, but it's too late. I'll always get the stories second- or third-hand, will miss the references and in-jokes but, however hard I or they try, I can never catch up.

It's another unhelpful thought that spins around in the high-speed blender that is my relationship with Robin. But, as the hot summer months would sadly attest to, sooner or later the spinning has to stop – it's just a question of how.

IX

RUNNING AGROUND

Walking on my sore leg.
Part one.

Robin

It's January. It's hot and I'm still busy. Jason and Matilda's wedding, which went smoothly, is over but family problems persist and so does the sciatic-nerve pain in my leg. In an environment of burn out, the smallest spark can kindle a fire, and tensions arise between Susannah and me over the dumbest things.

I had gone into the city for a lunch with friends and was travelling home on the train. Chatting on my phone, I missed my stop; suddenly I looked up to see Merlynston station, where my car was parked, receding behind me. I alighted at the next station and had the choice of waiting for a return train (boring), or walking back along the picturesque bush path beside the railway line. My leg was certainly not completely better, but I decided on the latter option. I had to pause a few times in the course of my little journey, but I reached my car none the worse for wear, having enjoyed the walk in the pleasant weather.

Recounting this to Susannah, she expresses her opinion that it was perhaps an unwise choice, given my injury. I assure her that it was fine and that probably the scrap of exercise had been good for me.

That should have been the end of this very unremarkable story. Sadly, no.

It is the beginning of a ridiculous tussle that leaves us both irritated.

This was the gist:

'I don't think you should have walked on your sore leg.'

'It's fine – it was good; no harm done.'

'I don't think you should have walked on your sore leg.'

'It's fine – it was good; no harm done.'

Reprise …

Susannah thinks she is being solicitous and caring; I feel she is being stubborn and controlling.

Susannah

I can tell that Robin is cross at me but I can't really understand why. I was trying to show I cared, that I was worried that she might hurt herself again, but she doesn't seem to want that concern and clearly sees it as an intrusion. I have obviously overstepped the mark and gone into an area that is none of my business.

I feel sad. I thought I was showing a daughterly concern but she is telling me in no uncertain terms that it is none of my business. I need to watch myself, be more careful.

Walking on my sore leg.
Part two.

Robin

It's late at night and I am watching the Australian Open tennis on television. It's been a somewhat emotionally draining day. Susannah and I had a long and convoluted phone conversation; she was feeling insecure and I couldn't reassure her. I think we finished up okay though. I am tired and probably should go to bed, but it is very relaxing here on the couch.

Susannah

As I watch the tennis with Oskar, my mind is working overtime. Thinking over today's call with Robin I realise that I am, once again, getting out of hand, bombarding her with too many unprocessed emotions, calls and text messages. I begin to fret that because of this she is now tiring of me. You would think that someone who thinks they are bombarding a person with messages would refrain from sending another message. Sadly, think again.

Robin

Ping! It's a text from Susannah.

Susannah

Hello. I don't want to lose you, or irritate you or bore you by being too much all the time. Do you think I am? X

What is she talking about? But I don't want us to get involved in some crazy analysis right now. I'm tired and just want to watch the tennis. I text back.

Robin

What are you talking about? You seem to be going a bit mental. I'm watching the tennis which is really good but am nearly falling asleep xx

Susannah

I will leave you alone. I'm sorry you're tired

I don't want to drive you away

But she's not really sorry it seems and it feels like she does want to drive me away.

Susannah

Okay a final – and a bit mental – question: Do you think that you know me? Obviously not completely, but …

God help me!

Robin

More and more I know you.

Susannah

Me, or imagined me? Happy to talk if easier.

Susannah

?

Oh no! I didn't see her last message immediately and now I'm in bed. I'll collapse if I have to keep texting. I am dead tired. I send what I hope is a final text.

> No, darling, I'm exhausted now. Couldn't talk if I tried. Need
> to sleep. I suspect it would not be very productive now
> anyway – we'd just get lost in silly philosophical circles.
> Let's say 'night-night'. X

Susannah

I should know better, I should say goodnight and leave it at that. But I don't: I feel hurt by her 'silly philosophical circles'. Robin is just calling the shots – if she thinks it's silly, it must be silly. She is dismissing me, rejecting me and I resent her for it. In my selfishness I forget she is an elderly woman and a tired one. I punch out a cross reply:

> I actually didn't want to circle but did want help.

Robin

I hear the beep of another text coming through and feel like weeping. I do not have the strength to tap out more letters with my tired, fat fingers, constantly making mistakes and having to correct them – excruciating! Talk about 'Don't walk on your sore leg' – now she's making me walk on my sore leg!

Susannah

No reply. Now I am cross. I send yet another text I probably shouldn't.

> Forget it!

No x for her.

Robin

Another beep! I can't do it; I'll read them in the morning. I go to sleep.

The next morning when I read Susannah's texts they strike me as petulant and selfish, but I don't say this when I reply.

> Robin
> Morning, have just got your last messages. I fell asleep last night, I really was 'done' to use Emma's expression. How are you all today?

Susannah

I wake to the ping of my phone and read Robin's text. I am still cross with her and don't want to reply. I realise I am being childish and playing games, but I don't care and I don't answer – she can have a taste of her own medicine.

Robin

No answer from Susannah. This feels like punishment, quite painful.

Susannah

I know that Robin will be worrying that I haven't replied. I know she will take the non-message as a message and I'm fine with that. I am also rather preoccupied with a major issue that has blown up with my daughter, so I flip between concerned, caring mother and needy, sulky daughter.

I even begin to think about what would happen if I never replied – would she call me? Probably not, it always seems to be me who calls. But perhaps I can lure a phone call out of her? Now I send a text.

> Susannah
> All a bit sad here …

It works. Robin calls. I talk to her about what's happening and I apologise for my poor text behaviour. Her voice calms me and it's good to be able to talk through things. We are back on track – but not for long.

X marks the spot

Susannah

It's late January, and Robin and I get into yet another argument. I have had a slightly difficult day with one of my new family members, but it all works out well. I text Robin, looking for some reassurance, some comfort, probably even some praise.

And Robin replies via text:

That's wonderful.

That's it? And a touch oversensitively, I grant you, I see I don't even get an x at the end of the text. So, I reply.

Susannah
No x?

Robin

I'm a little surprised by Susannah's reply. In my head I said it with deeply heartfelt gratitude and appreciation. Oh my goodness, in retrospect I see how crazy this is, how out of touch I am with the electronic medium I am using. IN MY HEAD? Do I think

238

Susannah is a mind reader? All she has is two words on the screen, which could be heard – in her head – in many different ways. I try to explain, still with delusional faith in my unconveyed emotional intensity

Robin
Sometimes, in certain contexts, an x seems to trivialise.

Susannah
Okay I see what you mean but 'little me' stresses when they're not there because it might be that they're being withheld. Mental perhaps, but honest. (x)

Susannah

What are you doing, Susannah? Could you be any more needy? Then again, say what you feel, right? And slightly humorous perhaps with the 'x' in parenthesis – that should lighten things a bit. Wrong.

Robin
Mmmm it could become meaningless if compulsory.
Could we try a little more faith in the relationship do you think? xxx

Susannah
Are you frustrated with me?

Because I'm getting frustrated with you – and I'm sorry but the xxx is coming a little late now …

Robin
No. The limitations of texting. Just sharing thoughts and wanting to be real. Do you see my point at all?

Yes, I see your fucking point, Robin! I just said that – do you always have to think, Robin? Would it kill you to feel sometimes?

239

That's what I would like to say but even I know that would be crazy. I try something that I hope is more sensible, to explain myself in a way she might understand. Be rational, Susannah, be clear, no emotion.

Susannah
Yes of course. I understand that I am over-sensitive to signals
of rejection from you – that's why I referenced 'little me' and
am highly conscious of being too needy on that front and am
trying to rein it in. That said, had great but emotionally raw
conversations today and just needed to be in touch with you
– I think it's okay to need reassurance even if I get you might
be tiring.

I am happy with that. I have calmed down. I feel I have acknowledged my failings but also exposed my vulnerability. I am hoping I get some love back.

Robin
You did touch in and my reply was genuinely expressing
a deep appreciation and commendation of you which
I really thought an x would trivialise. No tiring or rejecting
involved – just a difference of sensibility in that instance.

Oh for fuck's sake! 'A difference of sensibility in that instance!' This is impossible – would it really be so hard for you to say, 'Yes, darling, I understand'? Do you have to press an intellectual case, win every argument?

Susannah
Okay fine don't know what to say but thought it better to say
this than nothing.

Robin
You are cross. We can talk about it later, I love you.

Susannah

Not cross – but it wouldn't be too terrible to show your heart would it?

Robin

Now I'm cross. I'm sick of these accusations and judgments just because I don't respond exactly the way she might like me to respond – I feel controlled, bullied.

I guess we treat one another the way we would like to be treated. If I feel hurt, I like reasonable explanations to allay my concerns. I'm more comforted by them than by emotional *there, there*s. I had better call her. I've had enough of texting.

Susannah

Robin calls. I take the call in the garden and leave a slightly concerned Oskar watching the tennis (the tennis seems to be the soundtrack to our arguments these days). Things start off okay but soon go pear-shaped again. I try to explain. I acknowledge I was being needy, I apologise, but could she see what I was saying? It seems not. Robin is being very logical (not at all what I need at the moment – it just plays cold and hard to me) and then, as I begin to react emotionally, she starts to get frustrated and her voice rises in anger. Her voice is harsh and mean and I hit a wall. I feel overwhelmed and upset and I hang up on her. I stomp back inside.

'Fuck this! I do not need this!' I shout as I slam my phone down on the kitchen bench.

Oskar has now moved from slightly concerned to alarmed. 'What's the matter? What's happened?'

'I don't know. We argued ...'

'Again?' asks Oskar.

'Yes, again,' I confess. 'But this time Robin lost her temper and got really angry. It was awful, she was mean, so I just hung up.'

Oskar doesn't say anything.

'Fuck this!' I repeat. 'I do not need this. She doesn't need this! Perhaps this is just too hard. Maybe we're done and it's over!'

Where has this come from? Suddenly it all seems much bigger than one argument, one phone call. Suddenly it feels like the fight you have when you are breaking up with someone. Is that what is happening?

Oskar suggests – sensibly as it's now nearly 1am – that we go to bed, and I agree. Then Robin sends a text.

'Just leave it,' suggests Oskar.

'I can't,' I reply.

'You can,' he says.

Now I feel myself getting angry with poor Oskar but instead I crumble a little.

'I can't,' I say. 'I just can't.'

I open the text.

> We are both upset now and we both seem to feel unheard
> and misunderstood. I shouldn't get angry. I apologise for
> that, I do really love you but I feel you won't believe me unless
> I show it exactly the way you choose to show it.

Susannah

Aaaaaaarrrggghhh! Apology and then the power kick. This is not going to stop. Part of me, a really big part of me, doesn't want to reply. I want to cry. I want to follow Oskar's advice and go bed. I want to wake up in the morning and see if I can do this any more. But another, smaller but maybe braver part of me decides to hang in there. I send Robin a text.

> I don't think that's fair – but am up for trying to talk through it
> one more time if you are.

Robin calls back and we begin to talk again. And then, both of us, seemingly learning little from the last call, take our positions again: me appealing for a little affection, her for some common sense. And then her voice starts to harden and rise again. She has lost patience and I have just lost it. It's all too much. I break. I burst into tears. I know it's childish but I don't care, I am simply done in.

'Okay, okay, just please don't be angry with me, Robin.' I plead. And then I burst into tears again. It's all too much.

Robin

Oh dear, this is awful. I feel stricken by her tears. I guess I haven't fully grasped, and taken into account enough, the reality of the little baby Susannah I am dealing with. I was trying to talk adult-to-adult when it was completely inappropriate. I suppose I should have just dropped it and given her what she needed. Oh well! Another mistake to try to correct and recover from.

Susannah

Robin's voice softens and we somehow nurse the conversation to a vaguely reconciled end. I go to bed tear-stained and exhausted. Oskar stirs and puts his arm around me.

'Are you okay?' he mumbles.

'Not really,' I answer.

'Is this really worth it?' he asks.

I don't answer because I don't know. I thought I did but I don't anymore. Maybe Robin and I have just broken up.

Crossed wires

Susannah

When I wake up the next morning. I'm not angry anymore. I just feel sad and I start churning the argument of the night before over in my mind. I end up writing another poem. I write this and text it to Robin:

> I feel like we drove a bulldozer over our hearts and I'm sorry for my part in that. Hope we can heal the bruises …

> *You lost your temper*
> *And I lost the plot*
> *And we broke it*

> *A single x undoes us*
> *Too strong, too fragile*
> *Too much with too little*

> *Cry amongst the pieces*
> *Sifting heart debris*
> *Fear both fix and flee*

But the heart's battle song of open
Holds you to the path but with no map to find
Where X should mark our spot

Robin

What a sad and beautiful poem! She really is brilliant. But fragile. I think sometimes I am fooled by her natural ebullience into thinking she is more robust than she really is.

I send Susannah a text:

Darling I am so sorry. Please forgive me for crushing your heart. I love you. We are not broken, just badly bruised. We will find our special X. Meanwhile, please accept these tokens – xxxxxxxxxxxxx

The next day, Susannah comes over and we sit together with the cryptic crossword. Once again, it does its job. Where words have got us into trouble, here words help us out again: gloriously external, neutral words, carrying no emotional burdens; just the companionable pleasure of solving problems that don't actually matter. Frustrations and misunderstandings have all but run us aground but there is, after all, an X marking the spot to guide us to a calm, safe cove of respite. Crossed wires – cross words – CROSSWORD!

Susannah

But some things do matter and I wonder if we can heal the bruises. We seem better able to inflict new ones on each other at the moment and each argument chips away at my confidence and my energy.

And then, to add injury to insult, I find out I need to have shoulder surgery. That will mean hospital, a week to recover from the surgery and then at least three weeks with no driving. That alone is going to cause a lot of disruption to family life but also, I realise with panic as I come out of the surgeon's rooms, it will mean no driving to Robin's house. Would she come to me on the other side of town? Would she drive over? Might she even come and help look after me in that first week? I move from feeling panic to feeling quite taken with the idea: Robin seems to value acts of service as a way of expressing love – perhaps asking her to look after me is a better way for her than me banging on about leaving an 'x' on text messages all the time.

I ring Robin and tell her about the surgery. She is very sympathetic but when I mention the no driving and the idea that she might come to my house she pauses.

Robin

My first reaction to Susannah's suggestion that I drive to her house in Brighton for the next month is slight panic: I can't, I don't know how to get there, what will it involve?

This tends to be my initial reflex any time I don't know what exactly I may be committing myself to. I think 'No' – and then very often think 'Actually, yes, I probably can', a very short time later. Like the phone call with Maddy to arrange my first meeting with Susannah: 'No, I can't possibly do this Tuesday; it's too short notice … okay, we'll make it Tuesday.' Or when Susannah first suggested my staying overnight at Longleaf – maybe even for more than one night – 'Oh, I'm not sure, and if I do come, definitely not for more than one night.' I stayed four nights.

I have to weigh things up first.

Susannah

'It's quite a long way to drive,' she offers.

'Well, not really,' I reply, taken aback and thinking I drive to her place every week and it's about half the journey she makes to her church. It's a shot to the heart, but I press on. 'Maybe you could stay over, then?'

More pauses, more dodging and weaving. We agree to wait and see. She is clearly not enthusiastic and I am gutted.

Robin

I get off the phone and get out the Melways. Just holding this trusted old friend in my hands and feeling its weight and solidity anchors me with its promise of clarity and order. The basic first step of locating Susannah's street in the index at the back calms me further. None of your iPhones and GPS systems for this tortoise!

Already Brighton is a possibility – nay, even a potentially exciting prospect – I will be able to go to Susannah!

Susannah

I have hit a wall with Robin. Indeed, I feel like we are both bashing our heads against a brick wall, lots of brick walls, all the time. Maybe Robin is tired of it and that's why she's hesitant about coming to see me. Maybe she wants a break and this is her way out?

With not much in between, I go from being hurt to angry. I decide I am going to get in first: I don't think I can take Robin rejecting me. Perhaps I should step out, really out this time.

We just don't get each other – we barely speak the same language. She feels I am bullying her into being someone she isn't and I feel she just doesn't want to give me what I (both inner child and adult) need and what I so easily think she could.

We both seem tired of trying and tired of getting it, each other, wrong all the time. Yes, there's absolutely a connection, primal and strong, but it's perhaps not enough to take us the distance. We don't seem able to convert it into a real-life relationship.

Perhaps it is time to unhook? Something has to give. Or do we just give up?

X
SALVAGE

Searching for stillness

Susannah

Following the last phone call with Robin I am, once again, all at sea and at a loss to know what to do with my relationship with her. I desperately need to get a grip on something, ideally me. So, once again I hit the meditation cushion.

More often than not a good thought – albeit one I'm not supposed to be having – comes to me on the cushion, and so it is now. There I am trying to focus on my breath as thoughts tumble across in front of it. I replay the arguments with Robin, I wonder what I am going to cook for dinner, I plot a plan to simply withdraw from Robin, I wonder how people manage to meditate for hours and, every now and then, I notice that I am breathing. And then, with crystal clarity, a better thought comes to me. I realise that these thoughts to cut and run from Robin are not me formulating a proper response – they are a reaction fuelled in no small part by my little friend, my inner child. I see for the first time that my urge to run away, my hurt-and-hide routine, is little me protecting big me but also punishing Robin – it is a sulk but it is also a test. Would she come looking for me or would she reject me? Again.

This is a reasonable fear, given her form, but it is a childish reaction and I need a grown-up response. So, what is that response going to be? Am I really going to cut and run? Am I going to call Robin and tell her that it is all too hard, that it isn't working? I can tell her that and go back to my life – which actually had been great.

Finishing with Robin would give me certainty but it wouldn't give me peace. And, anyway, who am I kidding? I have been acting like I have a choice in this. Yet now, as I sit not meditating on my meditation cushion, I see, quite clearly, that I don't.

Because I realise that every time I think that it's all too much, another thing, more felt than thought, stops me. This woman – for all the differences between us and the misunderstandings we have – gets me. While there is a whole lot of stuff about me that she doesn't know yet, she fundamentally sees me and she can, when she wants to, make me feel unbeatable.

Just like – and it's only ever happened once before – Mum did. And that is the simple reality. I wasn't looking for another mother but now I have one anyway. It just is. That's a really special thing; amazing actually – lightning doesn't often strike twice, so you don't give it up easily. It's worth fighting for, even if you are fighting yourself.

I come across the quote from the Buddhist monk Chogyam Trungpa Rinpoche, 'The only true elegance is vulnerability' in a meditation book. This gets my attention, because I seem to be the pin-up girl for vulnerability – except for one critical difference: I have been seeing it as a bad thing. I saw it as putting myself out there – 'there' being a lonely, cold place where people might not come to find you, but this same place, the quote seems to say, is the only place you have a shot at genuine happiness. And then I pick up the Brené Brown book again and she is on about the same vulnerability thing: humans are wired for connection, belonging and love, but we need the courage to 'tell our own hearts'. That connection is everything but it isn't always easy.

You can say that again.

So, I have my light-bulb moment: I am never going to break from Robin. Even if she drives me nutty I am going to stay. I'm going to stop hiding when hurt, and I will stay out there in the open where she can see me. For better or worse, we are stuck with each other. It is no longer about if we have a relationship, it's just about how.

So, I ring Robin and ask if I can come over. I need to sort out this thing about her not being able to drive to Brighton.

Robin

Susannah comes to my house. We do our usual thing of getting our cups of tea and sitting out in the garden, but this morning Susannah is clearly upset about something. Finally it comes out that she is really hurt because she feels I don't care about her shoulder – or her, for that matter – because I just can't be bothered driving to Brighton to look after her.

I am mortified that she feels this, but I see now how she could quite easily have got that impression. I hasten to reassure her that that was never the case. I try to explain that sometimes when I am asked to do something I have an initial fear of incapability, but that it generally doesn't last long and I nearly always end up doing the thing. I tell her I want to come to her house and help her. I hug her and I tell her I love her. And it is true.

Susannah

I even get a hug. This honest vulnerability thing has a lot going for it. And then, of course, we do the cryptic crossword and everything feels better. But I do wonder if Robin can come out and be more open with her feelings as well: it has all felt a bit one-sided on the raw-emotion front.

I think I might have a cunning plan for that.

Eyes wide open

Susannah

I'm off to Robin's house for lunch and I am taking over a DVD of old family movies. I'm hoping that watching footage of me as a baby and toddler will provoke an emotional response from her. This is my biggest gun: if a curly-headed, fat-faced toddler doesn't get her, I don't think anything will.

Robin

Watching the old home movies seems a great idea, so we set ourselves up with cups of tea (hers always fresh mint; mine, your good old classic tannin variety) and settle cosily on the couch to enjoy the movies.

There is no soundtrack and the photographic quality is not always of the highest standard, but the general effect is that of a sun-bleached, idyllic world of childhood. The first scenes are in Susannah's grandparents' house in Toorak, with beautiful, extensive gardens made for exploration and adventure, and later shots showcase the family exploits on the tennis court and in the swimming pool. Everything is full of activity and fun – bikes, bats and balls, miniature-train rides. Everyone, especially Susannah's mum and dad, looks so invested, so happy.

There is Susannah as a toddler, probably about eighteen months, looking rather like a wind-up doll – golden curls, chubby legs, yellow frock – trying out her new walking skills, her mother following close behind, ready to rescue should it be necessary.

Suddenly, I am surprised by the feelings triggered within me: jealousy, resentment and a sense of ownership. *She's not yours, she's mine.* I have never thought or felt this before.

Such a dear little thing, eager and energetic – scrabbling up stairs, galloping at speed on the rocking horse, scudding along on an animal trolley of some kind, brandishing a toy gun.

Then watching her at about age five, I am struck by how much she resembled her sister Anna at the same age, not only physically but in personality, with a certain bumptious, I-am-great quality. (In fact, I can hardly believe it when the video shows her, at about nine, walking along making the 'V for Victory' sign with both hands, exactly as Anna used to do, accompanying the gesture with verbal brilliance of wit 'Thank, thank you, Fans and Air-conditioners!')

Despite this apparent healthy self-confidence, I can still see in the small Susannah that tentative quality that I had picked up in the later professional photo of her I had seen on the Net.

Then, quite suddenly, reality hits me.

It seems the veil that has been over my eyes and heart is suddenly removed and I see and feel, for the first time, the enormity of what I have done.

I gave away my best thing, my most precious treasure.

I have not always found it easy to give away, lose or break material objects that I have been attached to, but I had given away a baby, my baby!

This is the stuff of nightmares, those awful dreams where you belatedly realise that, in a moment of neglect, you have forgotten your child – left them on the train or at the shops. As the panic rises, you wake to the glorious relief that it is not true.

This awakening is the opposite: the realisation of a quite appalling fact.

I look again at the snapshots Susannah has given me of the 'little' her: an endearing nine-month-old fatso, her eyes alert with hope, then one of her about seven where she has an expression of vague puzzlement, like there is an unspoken question somewhere beneath the surface.

I see the disillusionment that must have hit that baby at birth. That astonishing and dismaying betrayal, *Where is my mother?* Again I feel the grief of her abandonment but now, for the first time, also the grief of my loss. I don't like it.

In this new light, I know without doubt that I made the wrong decision, but that was who I was then. I also believe that had I seen and held my baby, I would not have given her away.

I had asked the Lord to unlock my heart, to shine a light on the dark places of my soul – it seems He is faithfully answering my prayer. But light can hurt even while it heals.

Susannah

Well, Robin said I was cute, called me a 'dear little thing!', commented on how similar Anna and I were at the same age, and held my hand while we watched, but not much else. What was I hoping for? Tears? Definitely. An emotional outpouring? Probably, that would have been great. But at least some kind of realisation that it was a bit crap really, crap and sad and we could be sad together. Feel it together.

But no, not today. And I am out of ammunition.

Robin

Do I share my revelation with Susannah, here, sitting on the couch? No, I don't. It's too big, too raw; I have to carry it back to my private lair and try to come to terms with it by myself first.

So, I say, 'That was so interesting! Do you want another cup of tea?'

In my heart, I am grieving for my daughter and missing the lost years.

Missing the moment

Robin

Not long after the home-movie afternoon, Susannah shouts me the wonderful treat of taking me to see *The Lion King*.

We have dinner first at a little restaurant opposite the theatre and, once we have settled in with our usual easy rapport, I decide to share with her the revelation I had on watching the DVD of her as a child: how my heart finally felt the regret and the loss in giving her up for adoption. I put my knife and fork down and look at Susannah.

'Susannah,' I begin. 'When we watched your home movies I did have quite a huge revelation.'

Susannah looks up at me as I continue. 'I realise now that I had been given an enormously valuable treasure – and I gave it away. I gave away my baby.'

But Susannah doesn't say anything. I am talking from my heart but it is as if she doesn't hear me. I reach out and take her hand across the table. She smiles.

'That's really good, Robin,' says Susannah.

I may as well have said, 'I'm really enjoying the meal.'

It's strange how we all seem to be capable of missing the moment, and each other. Absent at just the wrong times.

Susannah

Now, finally, I get the reaction I want and I don't react.

In the middle of a busy restaurant, Robin tears up and tells me that now, after seeing those baby videos, she is sorry that she gave me up, that she now realises she had given away her most precious thing. That precious thing was me.

'That's really good, Robin,' I say. Did I really say that? It should have been a moment, an enormous one, and it wasn't, because I just let it pass. Inexplicably, even little me let it pass. We are both missing in action.

We finish dinner and walk across the road to the theatre. We watch a musical about a lion who has to work out who he really is – and I don't get that connection either.

In two days I will go in for my shoulder surgery – perhaps they can do my head at the same time?

Robin in Brighton

Robin

Susannah has had her surgery and I'm off to her place to look after her while Oskar is at work. I love this route to Brighton. I sweep smoothly on to the tollway, go across the Bolte Bridge with its view over the docks and the city centre, exit and wind through Port Melbourne for a bit before turning on to the coast road that takes me all the way to Brighton. The bay is exhilarating in all weather – sparkling in the sunshine or grey and windswept – but today is gloriously sunny. The road through St Kilda is lined with palm trees, the smaller of which resemble giant pineapples. I pass the old sea baths building with its green domes on my right and Luna Park on my left. I feel as if I am in a foreign country and I'm off on an exciting new adventure.

It is only when I come to the very last roundabout immediately before reaching my destination that confusion sets in and, virtually within sight of Susannah's house, I veer off in the wrong direction. (It turns out that this veering will happen on a fairly regular basis, leading me to the conclusion that the roundabout is bewitched. My daughter, who possibly suspects my poor sense of direction is to blame, rolls her eyes at this theory, but I am sticking to it.)

Susannah's house is a dark grey, double-storey building facing a park across the road; beyond the park is the beach. Inside, it is spacious and elegant, in the Scandinavian minimalist less-is-more style. I have been here once before, briefly, a few months ago, when Susannah gave me lunch after taking me to an appointment nearby. At that time, I had registered with some dismay the number of small Buddhas dotted around, but I have calmed down now over that issue, just as Susannah now accepts my talking to my 'imaginary friend'. While we both hold very different beliefs, we can now joke that we are both waiting for the lightning bolt of revelation to strike the other and wonder which one will be hit first. What could have been a big problem between us has worked itself out.

In fact, this time with Susannah at Brighton has made our relationship closer and better all round. I come in the morning and sleep over, which means I have been able to get to know Oskar and Emma better, which is lovely. Susannah and I ferry Emma to various appointments and pick her up from school. Sadly, Emma finds my bright blue car embarrassing in front of her peers, so this latter enterprise has to be 'black ops', as Susannah would say, and as soon as we have secured our passenger – who is shrinking down in the back seat – I must make a furtive getaway as quickly as possible.

The four of us have dinner together at the long dining table and the conversation is lively – most often Emma-led. My granddaughter (I'm still taking that one in) is a delightful girl: bright, creative, intense (No! Surely not!) and not afraid to speak her mind.

After dinner, we sometimes watch TV together, which is companionable and feels like family. Also watching TV – well, probably not actually watching it – are two other very important family members: the dogs, Bill and Bella. Bella is a Cavoodle, a woolly black bundle with a tongue. Unfortunately, she overuses this tongue, particularly by licking me enthusiastically on the face, which I just cannot find appealing even though I know it is well meant. For this reason, I prefer Bill, a small, elderly terrier who seems to lend himself to comparisons with movie stars, Susannah being convinced he is the spitting image of George Clooney, while I see a strong resemblance to Bill Nighy. Although Bella, who is Emma's favourite, undoubtedly has the sweeter nature, I must confess to a penchant for the wily, enigmatic Bill; it amuses me to look at him, and the lack of licking is a huge plus. Actually, they are both likeable rogues, who really only submit to Oskar, the master's voice.

Edvard, Emma's brother and a talented musician, I have yet to meet. I was tantalisingly close to a sighting one day when I was there and he had briefly returned to the family home to recover from the flu. But he remained upstairs, hidden from view, and I had to be content with hearing his footsteps overhead. So near and yet so far. The ghost who walks!

I have done my best to help the handicapped Susannah (who has her right arm out of action in a sling) with simple tasks in the kitchen such as chopping vegetables, lifting heavy pots and pans, making tea and coffee. I have also tried to arrange her bed pillows more comfortably, helped her dress, and rubbed her back. I have never had much confidence in my nursing skills, being rather clumsy with my hands (which is why texting is not easy for me), and I fear I take after my grandmother, whom we children nicknamed 'old stony hands'. But Susannah seems appreciative of my efforts nevertheless, which is gratifying: it makes me think perhaps I can mother her a bit after all.

We also go on some fun outings from Susannah's house, many of which reveal that Susannah – and Emma – have inherited the family tendency to immoderation. One afternoon, we rescue Emma from school – the dreaded science period – which is a bit naughty maybe, but nice as an exercise in biological bonding.

The three of us escape to the South Melbourne market, which offers an inviting array of delights for the free and feckless. Our first indulgence, for Susannah and me, is getting our faces threaded. I am so taken with my appearance afterwards that I bore my daughter and embarrass my granddaughter by declaring at too-regular intervals, 'I look stunning!'

Next, with gay abandon, we spend extravagantly on comestible treats including fresh oysters, Chinese dumplings and quaint candied fruit before hitting the Lolly Store, which dazzles with its variety and colour. By this time, the gene of excess is well and truly activated and we manically make our selections, catering (over-catering) to everyone's predilections, not forgetting to take home bags of licorice for Oskar. Indeed, no one is forgotten: Bill and Bella, we decide, must also be beneficiaries of our largesse, so after the lolly shop we seek out the pet-food shop. With discrimination long gone, we transition, without turning a hair, from purchasing our magical treats of fairy floss, Fantales and raspberry twirls to buying horrible animal things such as pigs' ears and kangaroo tendons.

Returning home with our diverse wares, we are tired (well, I am) but pleased with our afternoon's work. I call for the obligatory cup of tea, and retire to the comfort of the living room. I am joined almost immediately by Bill and Bella, who leap up beside me on the couch, nearly spilling my tea and basically totally invading my space. But I don't mind. In fact, I don't mind coming to Brighton at all.

Susannah

I have loved having Robin stay with us and I have loved having her look after me. For the first time, really, she has come into my world and I like that she seems to fit here. The fact that both Bill and Bella approve is an endorsement not to be taken lightly.

The cross-fertilisation of my new family members into my 'real' life increases when Anna comes over, soon after my surgery, bearing breakfast. It's crazy to think that a year ago I didn't know Robin or Anna and now they are both sitting on my convalescent bed eating croissants and doing the cryptic crossword with me. It's a source of great delight and wonder.

I have also been wondering about writing a book about this whole experience. As a writer I have furiously journalled my way through the past year but always for me, not for other people. Now I think that maybe there is a book in Robin's and my story. I talk it over with friends.

'You have to write about it, don't you?' asks one.

'You don't think you should finish living it first?' suggests another.

These are both interesting points. Robin and I are sitting at the back table at my house one evening and I ask what she thinks about the idea.

'A book?' she asks, looking more than a little surprised.

'Yes, you know,' I say, 'a book telling our reunion story, how we have managed to get through the hard stuff. It could be interesting, maybe even helpful to people.'

'Yes, I see,' she replies in a way that makes me think she doesn't. 'But why don't you write it? You're the writer.'

I plough on. 'Because it's *our* story and it would work better if we wrote it together.'

Robin continues to look unconvinced. 'Oh, no, Susannah, I don't think I could do that.'

I'm disappointed at her reaction but I have come to learn that Robin's first reaction isn't always – in fact, very often isn't – her final response. With an uncharacteristic patience I am trying to cultivate, I let the matter drop and we move on to another topic.

The next morning over coffee Robin brings up the book. 'You know, maybe we should talk about the book some more. It could be fun to write something together.'

I smile at her – I hope more with love than smugness. 'Okay,' I say. 'Brilliant!'

I begin to tell Robin some of the ideas I've had about the potential book and the two of us writing together. The thought of doing this is really growing on me but as it grows so too does another, much bigger thought alongside it, pushing something up I have been pushing down. If I have to tell my story to anyone, it is to my own family first – and to Dad.

Telling Dad

Susannah

It is now clear to me that it is impossible for me to continue to see Robin, to continue to become part of her life and the life of her family, and not tell Dad. And now that we seem to have decided to write a book together, any slight hope I may have been harbouring about keeping it secret is blown out of the water.

But it isn't just about the book. I now feel like I am having an affair. I am seeing or communicating with at least one member of my birth family most days and Dad knows nothing about them. And, increasingly, I am getting perilously close to lying. Dad will ring and ask what I've done that day, what my weekend plans are and, if they involve a biological, I dodge and skate around it, desperately trying to fall short of a straight-out lie.

One weekend Anna and her family come up to Longleaf, and Oskar and I really enjoy having them with us. When, on the Sunday night, Dad calls and asks what we have been up to, I answer merrily enough that we have been at the farm.

'Oh, lovely,' he replies. 'Did you have guests with you?'

Now I am stuck. I really, really don't want to lie. So, I don't. 'Yes, we did. Anna and Dominique and their family.'

'Anna and Dominique?' asks Dad, as if sifting through his mental Rolodex. 'I don't know them, do I?'

I hope that this will be that and we will move the conversation on. But no, we are staying with this topic and I am completely buggered.

'No, I don't think you have: they're new friends.'

But they're not, are they? Anna is my biological sister and I have just lied to my father. The last time I did that was when I was fifteen and, against Mum and Dad's express instructions, I had gone with a group of friends to Luna Park in St Kilda. I told them I was going into the city to see a film, which we had no intention of doing. We headed straight for Luna Park where we had a ball, possibly all the more for it being forbidden. But when I came home I was filled with guilt. I tried to forget about it but I couldn't and I felt awful. I eventually had to confess to Mum and Dad.

But not this time. I feel awful but I plough on and reinforce the lie. 'Yes, they're lovely. No, quite new friends. Have I not mentioned them before?'

And then it only gets worse – it isn't that the account of my weekend is false, it's that something enormous is going on in my life and I have failed to tell my father. I am lying by omission.

After confessing to the Luna Park deception, I had been grounded for a week. This time I also desperately want to confess but I fear much greater consequences. I believe, really believe, that Dad will be irreparably hurt and angry with me for making contact with my birth family. That he will see it as an enormous betrayal of my life family, of him and, particularly, of Mum. I fear he will reject me in return for what he sees as my rejection of him.

It really feels like I'm having an affair and I have only two options – tell Dad or stop the affair. I can't do either and so I'm stuck.

Robin

Susannah is really in a state about what to do with her dad – how to tell him about 'us'. She is so upset, she's not sleeping and I am worried it will make her sick. She is afraid of hurting him, and afraid of his disapproval and potential rejection of her. On the other hand, she feels terrible not being open with him, which of course I understand.

I try to sort the thing through with her. I suggest that she may well be projecting her own fears and hurts on to Brian, and also that she is reversing the parent/child roles, feeling it is her responsibility to look after him, much the same as I thought she did in her first letters to me. Of course, he should not be hurt unnecessarily, but he is a mature adult, responsible for his own emotions, and she is probably underestimating his ability to understand and cope with the situation.

I tell her that she will be honouring her dad by trusting him with her confidence – so much more than by allowing fear to shut him out of what is happening in her life. It's the same old story – real, intimate relationships involve courage and risk-taking. I suggest that writing a letter might be the way to go: easier to express herself calmly and clearly. Susannah agrees.

Susannah

When not being sponsored by Google, this whole relationship turns on letters. I write a letter to Dad but I am not going to send it: I am going to ask him to come over and read it with me.

With one final twist of the truth, I ring Dad and say I need his help with something.

'Of course, Susie, what is it?'

'I don't really want to say over the phone. Can you come over to my house?'

'Of course. When shall I come?'

'Tomorrow?'

'Oh, that soon?'

I can hear the concern now in Dad's voice.

'Yes, is that okay, Dad?'

'Yes, of course, darling.'

Of course he says it's okay – he's a good dad, and I'm about to let him down. Needless to say, I endure a shocking night of no sleep.

Brian

I spend an anxious evening fearing some very bad news. She's getting divorced? She has cancer? The family finances have collapsed? Then, as I drive to her house, another thought flickers across my mind: that it might be something to do with her adoption.

Susannah

As I welcome Dad with a kiss the next morning, I see that he looks nervous. We go into the living room and I don't even offer him a cup of tea: I need to get straight into it.

'I've written you a letter, Dad, because I want to tell you something but I want to make sure I say it right.'

'Okay,' he says. He has moved from looking nervous to alarmed. He gets his glasses out and begins to read.

Dear Dad

I'm writing this, rather than telling you because I am really worried that I will say the wrong thing and hurt you and I would never want to do that. You and Mum have been, are, the most important people in my life and I love you very much. I am so grateful for the love and care and opportunities, the safe and happy life you have provided for me, for all of us.

But something has happened that I have been scared to tell you about because I have worried that telling you will hurt you.

Over the last couple of months, however, I have been more scared that this something big in my life has happened and I have not shared it with you – it feels dishonest to keep important things from the most important people in my life.

That thing is that I have made contact with my birth mother and her family.

When he gets to this point. Dad stops and looks up at me.

'Oh thank goodness, I was so worried that someone was really sick. Oh, Susie, I'm so relieved. But, you know, I did wonder if it might be about this.' Then he reads on.

Dad, what I really want, need you to understand as you read those words is that there is no confusion that you and Mum are my parents and that I love you as my parents. I am so blessed to be part of our family. I would not wish my life, my family to be other than what it has been, what it is.

You know how you said it was wonderful how Mum seemed to speak to all of us just before she died?

And then he stops again. 'Yes, we each had our moment, didn't we? I was so pleased for that.'

To me, one morning when I was sitting with her, she opened her eyes in one of those moments of pointed clarity and asked, 'Did I do a good job, darling?' Well, what an easy question to answer. I told her she was incredible and that I loved her and was so grateful for her and she said she loved me. Mum was, quite simply, one of the most important things in my life – as with you, her care, her love, her support even when, most notably in teenage years, reciprocation was rare, has been unwavering. I am blessed to have landed in my family.

But I did come to my family, having been left by another and I think deep, deep down there was a wound. Mum told me once she thought we were a funny pair coming together – she grieving her daughters and me, in a primal, baby, way grieving my birth mother. Yet with her and your incredible awareness and love, we navigated and soothed our wounds.

Again Dad stops. 'Yes, you were very angry about all this when you were little. We did know how troubled you were. That's why we sought help for you.'

This is the only time I can remember talking to Dad about any of this. My heart feels less heavy as I realise he does get it. Dad reads on. I can see he is at the bit about Gwinganna and The Journey, about how it seemed to have prompted me to want to write a better letter than the one I wrote in 1989.

I did not want to write to my birth mother as a replacement for Mum, who is irreplaceable. I just wanted to write a letter with more empathy and warmth so that if she hadn't died my birth mother might feel more at peace, more forgiven.

And so I contacted the government department and, through them, sent a letter to my birth mother. I thought I was finishing things off, closing things but it seems I was actually opening.

She, Robin, replied and we began a tentative exchange of letters through the intermediary of the caseworker.

It became clear to me that I needed to meet her. I realised that I am genetically part of something else too. The unfinished business was also about me and who I am.

And, after a time, we met and, in time I met other members of the family.

At first I didn't tell you because I didn't think it mattered. I thought I was just writing this letter and that would be that.

When it turned out that it was starting something I wanted so much to tell you but I was scared.

I wanted to tell you so you could help me and so I could share it with you, my father, but I was so scared that it would hurt you and you would somehow think this meant I didn't love you and Mum as much as I do. I was, am, scared you would be hurt, you would be angry, and think that I was dishonouring you and Mum, our family.

But as time has gone on, I am more scared that I dishonour you and our relationship by not telling you. I feel like I'm lying by omission and that is a betrayal and disrespectful to you, to us.

Dad, my birth family does not replace my family. They are an addition to my life not a replacement, not a diminution of the wonderful thing I already have and value above all else.

Dad, I am scared that you will be angry at me, that you will reject me. I am scared that you will think that my desire to understand my genetic roots somehow weakens my bond to you and my family.

It doesn't but I do need you and your help to integrate my two realities.

I still have the letter you wrote me on my twenty-first birthday. You wrote: 'If I'd designed a daughter to my personal specifications, I don't see how she could have turned out better.' The same goes for you, Dad.

I love you.

Brian

As I read the letter Susie has written for me, I am at first slightly shaken, but only for a moment as relief takes over that it isn't any of those catastrophes I'd been preparing myself for. She feared I'd be angry but anger plays no part of my response and I am able to reassure her unreservedly. She's been a wonderful daughter and will, I know, continue so.

Susannah

Dad puts the letter down.

'So, you're not cross?' I ask.

'No, darling, of course I'm not cross. How could I be cross?' asks Dad, putting his arms around me. 'Mum and I have just always been so grateful to have you. All we have ever wanted is for you – all three of you kids – to be happy, and if this makes you happy, more complete, then that's wonderful.'

'Thanks, Dad,' I say, wiping my eyes, although thanks seems a far from adequate response.

Dad then asks some questions about Robin, and some questions about Tim and the rest of the family. I answer but am mindful to not go on and on: if nothing else I have learned that people need time to take things in.

'What do you need me to do?' asks Dad.

'Just know that it's happening and that that's okay,' I say. 'So I don't have to split into two.'

'Of course,' says Dad. 'I'll do anything you want me to, Sue.'

And of course he will. Because he always has. And it is wonderful. Dad is wonderful and I feel incredibly relieved. But there are two more important people who need to be told too – Sophie and Duncan.

Out in the open

Susannah

I decided to tell Sophie over lunch at Dad's house. I was nervous and anxious to get it over with so I cut to the chase soon after Sophie arrived. I told her, she listened, she said it was all fine. Yet as we sat down to lunch I looked across at my sister: after a lifetime together I can see when something is not right.

'All okay, Soph?'

'I'm not being replaced, am I?' she says. There is, I feel, a touch of a challenge. Fair enough.

'No, of course not! No one is!' I tell her. 'This is about adding, not taking away. It's about more love, not less. The heart has infinite capacity, I really believe that.'

And I do. It isn't just a line to reassure my sister, it's true. I'm not losing my family and they're not losing me – I have found more family and my heart has expanded to take them in. And I want Sophie to know that it will be okay. She seems satisfied and so we leave it at that, happily so, and talk about other things, the kids, life. And as I drive home from Dad's house, I realise that that was one of the best conversations I have had with my sister for some time – maybe this reunion is also bringing people together who were already there?

A few days later, I sit down to write my brother Duncan a letter for Dad to take over when he goes to stay with him in Cambridge. An email doesn't seem to be quite right and I don't want to call. The letter I write is similar to the one I wrote Dad, but without the fear. The email I find in my inbox one morning makes my heart sing: my brother says he is thrilled for me. I am grateful for his unquestioning support.

And I am thrilled for me. It looks like it's all going to be okay, I am going to be able to have it all, all the people I love. In my head, I update my dinner-party metaphor. Yes, I have arrived late and have shifted the dynamic of the room. I could get up from the table and leave or I could decide it's better-late-than-never and enjoy what's left of the night.

I have never been one to leave a party early and I'm not about to start now. I know what I am going to do – get up from the table, put on 'Dancing Queen' and ask if anyone wants my dessert.

So, with Robin's birthday party approaching, it's only fitting that I'm the one who brings the cake.

All in together

Robin

I will turn seventy-three in April and I want to have a gathering of family members, old and new. As many as possible, all together. Marian and Felix have offered to host the occasion and my daughters have volunteered to take over its organisation.

Susannah

We need to work out what we will have and who will bring what for Robin's party. As I seem to be slightly less busy, I email the other girls to outline some thoughts and ask for theirs. Anna emails back saying she thinks I sound very big-sister-like taking charge – and she is thrilled with this. I am chuffed because I have been a little worried that I am, again, overstepping my place. Jobs are allocated and I have, obviously, given my updated dinner-party metaphor, put my hand up to do the cake.

Robin seems pleased: after all the hard work she does for her family, she is enjoying being the one consulted not the coordinator, and I am happy we are doing that for her. She is, however, not very helpful when I ask what kind of cake she would like.

'Not too much fuss,' she says.

'But what kind of cake?' I ask.

'Vanilla,' she replies. 'But you know, just a packet cake.'

Baking is not a strength of mine. Cooking, yes, perhaps, but baking, no: I seem to fall down in the area of precision, which is, my baking friends tell me, everything when making a cake. I am more of the taste-and-throw school, which means my biscuits tend to bounce off the kitchen bench and my cakes never rise. Even the supposedly risk-free packet cakes, with built-in precision, have been known to come pancake-like out of the oven. So, baking I don't, but buying I do and I know the perfect place to purchase Robin's cake: an old-school bakery near home that specialises in sponge cakes. I set off to order it.

'A vanilla sponge for twenty people, please,' I say to the bakery lady.

'Yes, love,' she replies. 'Now, let me get my book. Here we go. Now, a vanilla sponge, good, and what colour icing?' she asks.

I freeze. I don't know Robin's favourite colour.

'Hmm, I don't know.'

'What's the birthday girl's favourite colour?' she asks, trying to help.

'I don't know,' I repeat, slightly testily. A hint of imposter syndrome floats through my mind as does a rejigged reprise of the Year 3 moment when my classmate cries, *She's not your real mother!* Pull yourself together, Susannah, it's just a bloody cake.

'White,' I say definitely. 'White with violet flowers and violet writing. "Happy Birthday Robin!" for the message. Please.'

The morning of the party, I feel a little anxious, partly because it will be the first time that Oskar and Emma are meeting everyone all in the one spot and also because that hint of imposter syndrome still hangs in the air. Anna rings and I confess my nerves to her.

'Don't be ridiculous,' she says. 'You are as much family as everyone else!'

She may not be completely right but I love her for saying it. We arrive just as Anna and her family are getting out of their car. Anna, the ultimate security blanket, gives me a big hug and we all go in together.

Robin

Marian and Felix's home is perfect for a party, with space indoors and out. Out the back, there is a generous timber deck from which a wide flight of stairs leads down to the garden. (These are the same stairs I tumbled down in my cane chair some months earlier.) The garden is large and country-like, and I particularly like it because it reminds me of my grandmother's garden in Western Australia, triggering nostalgic childhood memories. There is the dark green, spongy buffalo-grass lawn (again, typical to WA), long, rectangular vegetable plots burgeoning with autumn abundance, and a mysterious wilderness area down behind the gum trees and fruit trees, inviting exploration. There is also, at the back, an area paved with pink bricks, which has been adorned with coloured lights for my early-evening celebration. To add to the atmosphere, wood is being burned in a shallow rusty fire pit, redolent with the fragrance of eucalypt leaves.

So, already I am delighted by the environment, even before all these people who are dear to me arrive: my daughters and their families; Marian's sister Naomi and her family; Tim and Charmayne and their family, including Charmayne's sister and nephew; Susan, Florence (the sleuth) and her husband, Sam. Even a brand new puppy, Ned, acquired by Susan that very day, adds to the joy of the gathering. My vision of everyone being together is taking shape.

There is the usual convivial sharing of food and drink and small talk, and then the element of the Easter hunt is introduced – devised by Marian for the children as it is near enough to the seasonal festival to combine it with my birthday celebration. Marian has composed some extraordinary clues for the hunt, clever yet so cryptic they are unintelligible to the adults, let alone to the junior bounty hunters. To help the puzzled seekers in their quest, Anna decides that they need to be read aloud with accompanying dramatic actions. She nobly undertakes to perform this task and, taking up her position on the elevated deck, which serves as the perfect stage, she proceeds to entertain us with hammed-up and hilarious renditions of the clues. After each of her dramatic interpretations, the hunters dart off randomly to seek their chocolate fortunes, at times shamelessly aided and abetted by their parents, who have a vested interest in their success. Eventually, the hoards of bright and shining eggs are gathered, gloated over and many are immediately consumed. Fuelled by sugar, two of the youngest family members, Theo and Oliver, launch spontaneously into a synchronised vaudeville dance routine, which is most entertaining.

Susannah

It's time for the cake. Anna and I go inside to light the candles.

'You carry it out,' says Anna.

'No!' I exclaim. 'You do it.'

'But you should do it,' says Anna. 'You brought it and you're the oldest.'

Again, I love her for saying it but there is no way I am going to carry that cake out. I feel it would be presumptuous. 'No, really, Anna,' I beg. 'You do it.'

She concedes. We light the candles and head out on to the deck.

Robin

Then, there is more sugar – the birthday cake. Susannah has provided this, careful to discover my preferences and to cater to them meticulously. This attention to what may please others is one of her lovely character traits. Often she will turn up with something I have expressed a liking for in passing – a pot of special jam, elderflower cordial, certain flowers – or a kitchen utensil she has noticed the lack of. My cake is, therefore, of course perfect: vanilla with white vanilla icing, prettily decorated with edible flowers and multicoloured candles of an indeterminate number.

Anna bears the splendid creation out of the house to where I am seated, royally accepting homage. 'Happy Birthday' is sung with enthusiastic discordance and I blow out the candles to cheers and applause.

Then of course we must deploy the popper. This is a Chinese invention and one our family has adopted as an essential part of any celebration. You twist the end of a cardboard cylinder and release into the sky a rain of colourful and sparkling pieces of paper – magical! Poppers come in various sizes, but, of course, we always choose the giant size. Today, the honour of creating the magical effect falls to Marian and Emma, and truly the exuberance and joy they bring to this duty is a delight to behold.

Susannah

Prior to popping the popper, Marian gives an impromptu mini speech, in which she extols the wonder of 'the patchwork quilt' that is her family. It's a brilliant metaphor perfectly capturing the many different shades and threads in this family, with half-sisters and half-brothers everywhere. Except – and this is the thing I am learning about my biological tribe – no one ever calls anyone a half-sister or half-brother; in fact, there is nothing half about this family at all. Nothing half-hearted about anyone – every one is full, everything is full-on. Full-hearted.

As indeed, is their competitive spirit. Popper popped, Marian now produces a pink ball, and a game of volleyball of sorts is begun by some of the younger ones. Looking on, Oskar and I worry that our daughter's competitive spirit may be a bit overbearing. There is no need: it seems Emma too has found her tribe as they all fight each other fiercely for the right to control a small pink bouncy ball.

Panting, Emma takes a break to one side. 'They're just like me, Mum, aren't they?'

I smile. 'Yep.'

Over the top

Robin

Our family is always, for better or worse, full-on. On my side, it is, maybe, the combination of Irish and Latin blood that is to blame. My dad, who was by no means phlegmatic himself, tried to balance and manage his household of four highly strung females by quite regularly citing the motto 'Moderation in all things'; but the familial wild horse of extremes was not easily bridled.

What other clans might have called raging arguments, we called 'discussions' (though later we did begin to refer to these altercations as 'bushfires', indicating that some small amount of self-awareness was creeping in). No wonder Susannah, whose upbringing was much more 'English', meaning self-controlled, was dismayed by any show of anger on my part: she was not used to it and it frightened her.

We brought the same lack of restraint to pursuits of pleasure in my childhood. If we girls went shopping and liked more than one dress, for example, it was never a dilemma – just buy the lot. And we knew how to roister with gusto. Our house in Peppermint Grove was jokingly dubbed 'The Leuba Tavern' and friends from more reserved households were drawn to the comparative warmth and freedom it seemed to offer.

There was – and is – also nothing moderate about our use of language, hyperbole coming naturally to us. Nothing is just 'bad', it's 'hideous'; rarely is anything simply 'good', it's 'bliss'. My sister Susan, who has little interest in or aptitude for fixing things that are broken, instead encourages this activity in others by hailing the tightening of a screw or the switching on of a power source with cries of, 'Engineer! You're brilliant, a genius!' When it comes to anything technological, such as computers or mobiles, whole new levels of superlative praise are reached: whoever has plugged in the computer or accessed voicemail is proclaimed with awe to be a magician.

For my birthday, I receive some lovely gifts, but here again the principle of hyperbole must be adhered to. The reception of a present with anything less than raving appreciation – any mere 'Thank you, I really like it' – elicits an expression of horror on the face of the giver and a barrage of paranoid accusations: 'You don't like it! You hate it! Why do you hate it?'

While Susannah shares some of these hyperbolic tendencies, she has also brought to the table her own speciality: the neurotic obsession with the obligatory addition of kisses (xxx) to any written communication. Her new family members, who did not formerly strictly adhere to this practice, have now been trained in the custom to such an extent that should they realise they have pressed 'send' without the compulsory 'xxx's, they are struck with guilty fear and quickly correct.

Due to the fact that Tim is her father, hooking her up to a whole new pipeline of Scottish/American madness, Susannah has inherited a double portion of the gene of excess, especially in the realm of roistering. For her, every anniversary or celebratory occasion must ideally be extended into a Festival, ranging over at least a week. Hence there was no way my birthday party at Marian's, excellent though it was, could possibly be the end of the story. Knowing I like seafood, Susannah immediately commissioned a seafood dinner to be held at my house, incorporating a sister sleepover. The bland word 'dinner' was soon disposed of, quickly becoming 'seafood bonanza'; still unsatisfied, Susannah then pronounced it to be a 'seafood extravaganza', thereby giving licence to the full expression of the aforesaid gene.

On the evening of the extravaganza the girls all come bearing cornucopias from Canals Seafoods: oysters, lobster, calamari, prawns. It is all absolutely delicious – and of course ridiculously abundant. My last image from the dining table is that of a colossal mound of crustacean remains, quite grotesque in their post-prandial state.

We flee this scene of carnage and adjourn to the living room, where tea and coffee are called for. This service falls traditionally to Marian who, as the youngest, was early co-opted into small acts of slavery by her older sisters.

We drink our beverages, chat, and then, of course, get out the cryptic. Marian, for reasons known only to herself, has for some time eschewed the Australian papers, including *The Age*, in favour of the English *Guardian*. She is, therefore, not conversant with the quirks of the local crossword composers and protests at the difficulty of the exercise. We assure her that she is not dumb, just deprived of adequate tuition. We offer our services, but will she have the motivation to persevere? After all, *The Age*'s cryptic crossword is not everyone's universal panacea.

Mattresses are set up on the floor of the living room for the sleepover, but despite the fact that this is totally in line with my childhood vision of the giant bed, I do later defect from the cause and retreat to the comfort of my own single bed, leaving the young ones to the cosy clump. At seventy-three, I'm just a bit past the cosy clump – in a physical way, at least.

My birthday festival is declared officially over at midnight when I, Cinderella-like, surrender my position of honour and revert to the status of servant, having been commanded to report for duty in the kitchen the next morning to cook breakfast: eggs, bacon and Johnny cakes, the latter a family tradition passed on to me from my mother, Florence. So, in the morning I am Mum again, and very happy to be so.

The offspring leave and I sit down at the dining-room table with paper and pen. It's time for me to apply myself to the writing task that Susannah has set me for our book: the account of my pregnancy and Susannah's birth in 1965. I have said to Susannah that I can't really remember anything but, as I start to write, the words flow easily and, it seems, I remember more than I thought.

Once more with feeling

Susannah

Robin and I have decided we will give this 'book thing' a go and have begun writing pieces from our different perspectives to see if they might build up into a story. Robin has emailed me her writing about what happened in 1965. I start reading. I am not worried, I am excited: I am in work mode and, after all, I know this story, I've heard it all before, so it will be okay.

Right? Wrong.

As I read, my heart pounds, my chest tightens and I feel lost all over again. I am as irritated as I am distressed: I thought I had this stuff all sorted out now. What's going on? I call Robin and I tell her that her writing is beautiful but that her piece has really upset me. She tells me that she is sad that I am sad and we agree that we are both confused by what's happened – perhaps this book is not such a good idea after all?

I continue to churn and, later that evening, I send Robin a slightly, only slightly, mental text. She responds lovingly but briefly and I know she is tired. I text back a goodnight message: at least, I think to myself, I have learned not to spam my elderly birth mother late at night – and she has learned to let me know gently when she's tired and can't talk anymore. But I continue to churn.

And then, after a few more churns, I get it: something shifts. Maybe, finally after nearly a year, the adult me has worked it, or at least enough of it, out. But I realise that little me, the sad baby, whom I no longer think of as pesky but in need of protection, hasn't worked it out yet. She's not thinking, she's just feeling and she is still angry – really angry – and confused. Little me needs big me to help her. So, I have a chat with her and I promise I will speak for her and I will tell Robin how she feels. She will have her moment to be heard. Better late than never, I tell her.

Little me likes this a lot. Can we really tell her what we think? Can we really say anything? Yes, I reassure her, we can say anything, we can give her hell if we want to, and it will be okay. I promise her.

I also promise that there will be no 'good girl' attempt to understand Robin's side of the story, no 'Gosh it must have been difficult for you too,' or 'But it's all okay because look how it turned out.' The baby wants its moment of pure, uncompromised anger. And, after fifty years, I reckon she is entitled to it – indeed, I need her to have it so I, we, Robin and I, can move on and have a relationship that looks forward not back.

So, my inner child and I sit down and together we write a reply to Robin's 1965 piece. It's pretty full-on but I, we, decide to give it to Robin tomorrow, to let her have it.

Robin

I am off to Susannah's house. There are no particular plans for the day but I am looking forward to seeing her and perhaps talking more about our book idea.

Susannah

Poor woman, it's going to be like an ambush. She doesn't know what I'm about to do to her; she thinks she's coming to spend a lovely day together. I see her car pull up and my throat dries; I feel sick knowing what I am about to do but I am also determined.

Robin comes to the door and I greet her with a hug. She seems to immediately sense that something is not right.

'Susannah, what's wrong?'

We go into the living room. I don't offer her her normal cup of tea.

'Um, you know how I got upset reading your 1965 piece?'

'Yes.'

'Well, I've written a response to it. We actually.'

'We?'

'Can you just read this?'

I give Robin the first page.

When I read your 1965 piece I went mental – yes, I know – again. I'm sorry but at least now I think I have worked out the problem.

Fifty-year-old me does get it, understands 1965 – balances it with 1989 – says 'okay, let's say we're even' – and forgives. She thinks 'let's enjoy now, the clicks of connection, the energy and pull of the genetic magnet.'

But little me, the howling baby, the lost toddler, doesn't get it yet. She is still angry, really angry and confused about you – but she is so happy to be back, reconnected whence she was ripped that she doesn't dare say that – because then you might leave her all over again. So, she'll say anything, including that she forgives you, to make sure you stay.

But this is what she really wants to say …

Robin looks up at me.

'Okay?' she says, shakily.

'Are you up for reading the second page?' I ask quietly. 'It's pretty full-on.'

'Yes,' says Robin without hesitation.

Of course she's up for it, she always is. I watch her as she reads it and she starts to cry.

We've responded to your 1965 piece.

<u>*1965 – you*</u>
I could hear my voice, strangely detached from me, roaring in the drugged darkness …

I returned to Perth, where I resumed my life and my relationship with Tim, and buried the whole experience deep within my subconscious. In general, I tend to be a bit of a blabbermouth, not the soul of discretion, but the fact that I had adopted out a child was my one dark secret. It lay undisturbed for twenty-four years.

<u>*1965 – me*</u>
Well, lucky you, undisturbed.

Not me.

I am disturbed, distressed, desolate the moment they pull me from your fraudulent womb.

Oi! Anyone! Where is my mother?

At least you were drugged – nothing dulls my roar – I scream and scream and scream while you resume your life.

I throw up the milk they try to feed me and there is nothing to numb my pain as I arch and clench in raw hurt, anger, confusion and loss.

No one explains the 'no bonds' policy to me.

It is fucked, completely fucked – and it is your fault.

Your dream is my nightmare.

Someone else cleans up your mess.

And I give up on you.

So, by the time you finally decide to wake up, it is way too late.

Robin

I read what Susannah has written. Really, she is just the agent, the go-between, faithfully delivering a message from my baby, Florence Leuba. It's taken fifty years to get to me, but better late than never.

Each line falls on me like a blow to the heart – and each one I fully receive with no resistance, no remonstrance. Because the case against me is true and it is my fault. It is crucial that I own it and take the pain of owning it. One excuse, one 'fig leaf' of self-justification will close the door on the opportunity for healing. My baby needs and deserves pure, uncompromised recognition of the wound inflicted on her; she needs her sorry day.

I tried to say 'sorry', to ask Susannah's forgiveness, right back in the first letter I wrote in 1989. But I saw in her reply that she didn't get it then: she was in unconscious denial of her wound and said, and believed, she had nothing to forgive me for. We have both done our share of sleepwalking.

She also had her illusion that I had wanted her but had been forced to give her up for adoption. This bubble was broken the day she walked out of my house. She was winded by the blow but quickly – too quickly – struggled to her feet. I again said sorry for the hurt I had caused her and asked for her forgiveness. At least this time she acknowledged with her head that I had wounded her and there was something to forgive after all – and she did forgive me – but her heart still hadn't really got it, hadn't felt the pain and the anger.

And finally it has: the comfort blanket has been taken away and she has let the full force of the cold wind of betrayal hit her. I feel it too now and I break down crying. I pull Susannah towards me and talk to her as I cry.

'I'm sorry, little Baby Leuba, for that betrayal. I'm sorry for the terror and confusion of abandonment that made you scream and vomit up your milk. And I'm sorry for both of us that I didn't just take you on my breast and take you home. I'm sorry, little toddler, for the legacy of unsureness showing in your eyes, for the scars on your tender little heart. I'm sorry for our mutual loss. I'm sorry, I'm sorry.'

Susannah

We are both crying now as we sit together on the sofa. After a while, I lift my head up.

'I think it must have been awful for me, that little baby,' I say.

'Yes,' says Robin, stroking my hair. 'I really am sorry, Susannah.'

And then we sit there some more, just letting things sit, sink in.

'Robin?' I ask after a while.

'Yes?'

'Time for the cryptic, do you think?'

'Definitely.'

And once again, thank her God, we've made it through. We sit together, solving puzzles, talking and laughing in between the clues and healing.

A few hours later, Robin has gone home and Oskar, Emma and I pick up Edvard and we head off to the launch of Dad's new book. Dad's book launches are legendary, both in their frequency and their joviality. He makes writing look easy (although those close to him see his effort) and public speaking even easier. His book launch speech is witty and generous, and I listen and laugh with admiration. As I look around the room of people also listening and laughing, I realise how warm and familiar everything and everyone is. Here are the people whom I have known, and been known by, all my life: family and friends of Mum and Dad's who know both my trials (and those I've put my parents through) and my triumphs, and have supported and celebrated me through all of them.

What a completely weird yet wonderful day.

And it finishes, post-launch, with a dinner with Dad, Sophie's family and mine. We sit down, we order, we toast Dad and we talk – with each other, over each other, just like families do. At one point, Dad turns to me.

'What did you do today?'

'Oh, not much,' I reply. 'I told Robin that she had inflicted a deep and primal wound on me by giving me up and that my inner child was seriously pissed off at her.'

'Oh, really?' replies Dad. 'How interesting. How'd that work out? Can you pass the garlic bread?'

Well, the last line happened anyway. There was no need to tell anyone else about what happened earlier – it was huge but it was just between Robin and me.

Maybe, now, I have finally got my head and heart together?

'Heart attack'

Robin

Susannah is at my place to have a day of writing together for the book, which we have decided to call *Heartlines*. She has slept over the night before so that we can make an early start and ACHIEVE! For me especially this is important because my working window of opportunity is relatively small. I must take advantage of my brain when it is fresh, before the blind of mental fatigue is pulled down and it virtually shuts up shop. No negotiation, not interested in overtime.

The day begins well. Susannah goes for a dawn run in the cemetery, as is her wont. I am blessed to live close to a very large memorial park, Fawkner Cemetery, which is quite beautiful. It affords the visitor (and the permanent residents) green sweeping lawns, grand and gracious avenues of trees, rose gardens and swathes of different coloured daisies tumbling over the spaces between the graves. Some parts of the park are formal and elegant; others are wilder and more Australian and you really feel you are in the country. This impression is reinforced by the fact that bunnies abound, springing away in front of the walker, while white cockatoos swoop and soar with their mad squawking cries.

When Susannah of the boundless energy returns from her run, we decide that before applying ourselves to our writing task, we will do the cryptic over a cup of coffee and then have breakfast. Sitting together on the couch, we embark on our cosy word-mulling and are sailing along nicely when the unthinkable happens – we have a stupid argument over the cryptic. Same old ridiculous story – crossed wires of communication. Irritated with each other, we don't say much, but continue our efforts with the crossword, albeit with slightly less joy than usual.

Then, as I start preparing the grilled tomatoes, Susannah feels a sharp pain in her chest. She says it is probably nothing and sits down and waits for it to pass, which it does. It is a lovely sunny morning and after breakfast we take a walk together to further clear the air of any lingering negativity. So, it is off to the cemetery again for us.

We stroll along the pathways, enjoying the warmth of the sun, stopping to read inscriptions on the plaques and gravestones. We have been walking for about twenty minutes when Susannah starts feeling peculiar: fuzzy in her head and exhausted. Clearly this is not good and we make our way home as quickly as we can – which is very slowly. On arriving back at the house, she doesn't even take her coat off but just lies on the couch saying, 'I just want to go to sleep.' With thoughts of people lost in the snow who succumb to the temptation to lie down and sleep forever, I persuade her into the car and I drive her to my doctor.

On examination, her blood pressure (which apparently has always been excellent) is found to be dangerously high. The doctor is concerned for her heart and advises we go straight to hospital where everything can be checked with greater efficiency. The ambulance is called and Susannah waits on a bed in a side room for the arrival of the paramedics. It is always a shock when, out of the blue, the program of the day is blasted away and one finds oneself in a different space altogether. Who would have imagined a few hours earlier that I would be standing in that neutral little room looking at my daughter lying on a bed with a possibly serious heart problem? I feel like I am in a capsule outside of time, with the pause button having been pressed on normal life.

Fear tries to get the better of me, with thoughts of Susannah dying – that awful feeling in your chest: simultaneously a gripping and a melting, sort of like you are a stone beginning to dissolve.

I try to appear calm for Susannah's sake and I take appropriate practical actions: I ring Oskar and tell him the situation: he is, of course, worried, and I reassure him I will ring back as soon as I know something. I then ring Susan and ask her to pray and to ask my prayer partner, Ilona, to pray too.

Then we wait.

Susannah

I am taken to a treatment room to wait for the ambulance. I all but collapse on the bed: I am exhausted and feel strangely other, outside myself, and desperately want to sleep. But I can see that the doctor looks worried, and that worries me. He tells me that he is concerned about my soaring blood pressure. I tell him that I don't get high blood pressure. 'You do now,' he tells me. He thinks that I might be having some kind of heart attack.

Heart attack? Is this going to be it? No! I am not ready, I still have things I want to do, things Oskar and I want to do, and the kids need me a little bit longer at least, I certainly can't leave them yet. And I don't want to die here on this bed. My mind lurches now and I am scared and none of this is good for my blood pressure, which continues to soar. I look across at Robin, who also looks worried, and I am struck by the potential symmetry of the situation.

'Robin?' I say.

'Yes, darling?' she says as she comes over and takes my hand.

'I'm a little scared.'

She doesn't say anything.

'Do you think it's going to be that you are with me at both my beginning and end?'

'Don't say that,' she says and squeezes my hand. 'It's not going to happen.'

I am less convinced.

Robin

The paramedics arrive and hook Susannah up to various monitors. Her blood pressure is still high but they bring a note of optimism by saying she does not present like a typical heart-attack patient, of which, sadly, they see many. However, it is still an anxious and somewhat surreal ride in the ambulance with her to the nearest hospital.

When we arrive at the emergency department, the back doors of the ambulance are opened and I alight. At that moment a call comes through on Susannah's mobile, which she answers. I can't help but see the comic irony in Susannah raising herself from her stretcher and, still trailing monitor leads to her heart, announcing that we have secured a publisher for *Heartlines*. This is news we have been hoping for and that normally would have been received with excitement and the immediate instigation of a festival of celebration. As it is, I barely register the happy fact – it is so not a priority in the present circumstances. How often things turn out differently than what we imagine.

Once inside the hospital, Susannah is wheeled into a cubicle and I deal with the red tape at the reception desk.

'So, you are her mum?' the girl asks.

'Yes,' I reply, savouring the fact of it, as a newly married couple might secretly savour the novelty of the labels 'husband' and 'wife'. Again, when the doctor sits in the cubicle with us and talks of family and childhood history, naturally assuming I have raised Susannah, it is as if, for that short time, I can actually be that mother. I enjoy the fantasy.

Susannah

I have wires stuck on everywhere, I have had my blood taken and a chest X-ray done and now I lie here, with Robin sitting next to me while the nurse asks me questions. Then she asks whether there is a family history of heart conditions. I am about to say what I have said for fifty years – that I don't know – when I realise that I do now, I can.

'Robin, is there?'

'No,' she replies.

I am not sure what makes me happier: that there is no family history of heart conditions or that I can finally answer those medical questions.

All tests for anything serious come back negative, but the doctors recommend that I stay close to the hospital that night. I call Oskar to reassure him and tell him I will stay at Robin's. He, of course, wants to come and see me but I suggest it's crazy to drive all the way across town in peak hour traffic to see a completely well, if now exhausted, wife. He reluctantly agrees.

Robin

That evening I can enjoy a mother's reward: the amazing feeling of relief that the child is all right.

Probably one of the most defining characteristics of a mother is that she goes through inevitable times of anxiety over her children, because they are the ones she can't afford to lose. As someone has said, having children is like having your heart walking around outside your body. A mother is always vulnerable through her children. This experience with Susannah has bonded me to her in a new way and I realise that I do indeed now have another person on whose happiness my own happiness depends.

Susannah is tucked up in my special old-person's massage bed with a hot-water bottle and herbal tea. I sleep in the bunk bed and revel in the fact that we are both safe and sound.

Return to Gwinganna

Susannah

It is, obviously, a huge relief not to be having a heart attack but the leaping blood pressure was clearly my body trying to tell me something. Throughout all the stresses and distresses of the past years I have never had a problem with blood pressure and yet here I am flipping it up to dangerous levels because I had an argument with Robin over the cryptic crossword!

But of course it wasn't just the stupid argument over the crossword – although it was sad that our once impenetrable refuge had now also fallen – it was everything, good and bad, just stacking up on top of me, and now my body, both heart and head in collusion, is saying enough already, give us a chance. Just as I think I have done all the hard work of opening up – acknowledging the pain of my abandonment to Robin and coming clean with Dad – my body is closing. I have to do something.

So, I decide to take myself back to Gwinganna, the wellness retreat that seemed to have started all this.

Friends and family, unsettled by my 'heart attack', think the retreat is an excellent idea, but everyone, without exception, has one caveat – under no circumstances am I to take 'The Journey' again.

'You're not going to do The Journey, are you?'

'I don't think that Journey thing is a good idea, do you?'

'I have thought about doing it,' I say. 'Perhaps it will help?'

No, they all assure me, it will not. One friend even goes so far as to say that *she* could not cope with my doing The Journey and makes me promise that I won't do it. 'If you think you're about to sign up for it, call me. Immediately. I'm serious, Susannah. I really, *really* think The Journey is a bad idea for everyone.'

I agree and I promise, not without some guilt at the belated realisation that I have also put my friends through a lot this year.

I arrive at the retreat, at the top of a mountain, on a beautiful sunny afternoon. I check in and then see a consultant to book my treatments. As I talk to the consultant, my husband's and friends' pleas ring in my ears and I decide to stay superficial: a facial, a massage, I'm thinking.

The consultant booking my treatments clearly thinks I can do better.

'What do you want to learn about yourself here?'

'Absolutely nothing,' I almost yell, or maybe plead. 'Absolutely nothing more. I'm still recovering from last time!'

The consultant, realising she may be in the presence of a nutter, just smiles. 'Okay,' she says. 'Well, that facial will be just lovely.'

But then, as the week rolls relaxingly on, I decide to take one leap-of-faith treatment, something I wouldn't normally do. And one particular treatment seems to be calling me – Body Release. *Why not?* I think as I book myself in.

Waiting for the treatment therapist the next day, I expect an earth-mother type, possibly with the odd crystal adorning her, but, instead, a young, very fit-looking man wearing no crystals comes towards me.

'Right, mate, let's get you sorted.'

He explains that the idea is that my body is tested for areas of weakness, organ health, circulation and toxic build-up, assessed by a series of subtle chiropractic-like movements.

All is going well. I am, it seems, just like the emergency-room doctor confirmed, a perfect specimen of health.

'You're solid, mate,' he keeps repeating. 'Real solid.' He even wonders out aloud why I chose this treatment.

But then he gets to my brain.

He does one test.

'Ah,' he says. 'Let's check that again.'

He does it again.

'What's going on, mate?' he exclaims.

'What do you mean?' I ask, slightly alarmed. After all, no tests were done on my brain in the hospital.

'Well,' he explains, 'the one side of your brain, you know, your thinking part, has been working really hard. And it's really strong, solid, it's really good at processing stuff, but ...'

'Yes?'

'Your other side, your feeling side, it's all over the shop, mate, it can't keep up with all that stuff. You've got to give it time. You're trying to fix too much. You've got emotional indigestion.'

There it is. He has nailed it. Emotional indigestion is exactly what I have.

'Yes!' I exclaim nearly leaping off the table. 'I do! Can you fix that?'

'Yep, sure. I'm on it.'

And with that he put his hands at the back of my head and gently clicks it forward.

'Okay,' he said, lifting my arm up again. 'Push up when I push down.'

I obey and push firmly up against his hand.

'There you go, mate, all solid, sorted, you're good to go.'

'That's it?'

'Yep, you're solid, mate,' he repeats. 'We just needed to get that heart up to speed. Take it easy now.'

And so I walk out of the treatment room a little bemused: I don't know why I have been doing all this thinking over the past year when I could have just had this bloke click my head!

A bit later, a group of us are walking into the bush when we see a dove lying on the ground. It has flown into the glass windows of the gym and has been stunned, or worse. As we approach, the poor thing becomes distressed. We wonder what we should do. Try to help it or, more grimly but perhaps necessarily, euthanase it? Our guide has a thought: we could just leave it, see what happens. We decide to go with that and walk on. Minutes later someone calls out from back at the gym: 'Look, it's flying off!' And so it is.

I feel I am being told something: slow down, you don't need to dive in and fix everything. Sometimes just wait and see what happens.

The clicking perhaps, my little bird message and the time away do allow me to slow right down, to detox and digest the mental year that was the year I met my other mother. Long walks in beautiful bush, no caffeine, no alcohol, no sugar, calming, nurturing massages, crazy dancing, drumming to excellently daggy 1980s music, the odd bit of hollering in the rainforest and time to do nothing allows me to, finally, thankfully, fall into a softer, more spacious place.

One of the final seminars of the week is 'From Limbic to Prefrontal – From Reaction to Response' on how we need to get less limbic (our more primal reactive) and more pre-frontal (our more considered responsive), and everything I have read, meditated on, thought and felt comes into one neat little ball in my lap.

My lovely but mad limbic inner child had gone mental from the moment I began contact with Robin – the speaker talks of a 'limbic hijack' – and that reconnection had opened all the lost and repressed files of my birth experience and thrown them out of the filing cabinet of my mind, scattering them all over the floor.

So I cried out for maternal affection; I sulked and I danced as I tried to please both mother and all my other biological family because I wanted them to love me. And I tried to protect my life family from any pain, terrified that they would reject me, because I needed them to love me too.

I rushed and I raced, desperately trying to fix and fit in, all the while hurling my limbic files in a messy whirl. Then, like a cute but exhausted puppy, I crashed, falling down, depleted, among all the files.

But, the speaker continues, you can pick up those files and step out of your limbic reaction. You can choose not to follow it, you can choose where to focus your attention.

So, where do I want to focus mine? I ponder this all the next day and, finally, I write just six words.

Gratitude
Laughter
Openness
Vulnerability
Joy
Love

That love thing again, it anchors everything. And with love, more is more: more family, more people to love, more people to love you – it takes from no one, only adds. So, no more talk of 'biologicals' for me. No more 'life' family and 'blood' family. Just family. It's time to let go of the limbic, the worrying, the dancing to please. Finally, I am combobulated!

And then, on my last day, lying on a massage bed with the masseuse repeating, 'Let go, you don't have to hold this,' I finally do let go – I let go of a whole lifetime of held anger and hurt about what happened and, somewhat embarrassingly, I burst into tears.

'There you go,' the masseuse says softly.

I am ready to go home. I have finally got my head and heart together. But there is one more thing I need to do, one more thing to let go of.

XI

HOMECOMING

'Home is where one starts from.' T.S. Eliot

Robin

Elsewhere

Little honey-haired girl with the questioning eyes:
'Where did I come from? From beyond the skies?'

'You came from me, a part of me, but cut loose straightaway
before we could see – each other.'

Strangely adrift, though taken in; wanted and loved but not by
   your kin.
Wondering, puzzled: 'Where did I come from? Why here, not there?
Because I'm not from here – but elsewhere.'

Set out now to find that place: that other harbour that reflects
   your face.
To see, to know, to join at last – to tether your soul, to make it fast.

'Then out I can sail again, secure but free,
no longer "elsewhere", but Here and Now – Me'.

Letting go

Susannah

Back home, I place a photo of Robin as a toddler on my desk – it's there to remind me that she too has her own little limbic inner child banging on her adult door and because, contrary to most of my behaviour over the past year, I am an adult too and I need to bear that in mind. I need to see Robin as a person, not just my birth mother, who, at various times, has done my heart and head in.

And I need to move me, us, on from what happened in 1965 and 1989.

And so, I read Robin's book again but this time I'm looking for her, not me. I'm trying to understand her in her own right and life, not the role she has played in mine. It makes for quite a different read.

I see poor little Wobin Uber, the unsure schoolgirl who, like me, can't say *r* and who is humiliated in class, declared a crow rather than a nightingale (who does that to a child?) for her less than tuneful singing. I see a beautiful young woman who perhaps doesn't quite believe her own intelligence and strength – and who, maybe, looks to other people for validation. And I see a woman who loses a lot, who cops a lot of pain and many challenges – but who keeps standing.

I look at that photo on my desk – the toddler, cute podgy legs yet to walk off all their baby fat, standing on a chair in that paddock as if to say, 'Oi! I'm over here and I've got stuff to say. See me, I'm ace.'

And I do, and she is.

And then I Google forgiveness rituals. Because I've got stuff to say too.

I walk to the beach with Emma and we collect some stones, and then I sit down and write one final letter to Robin. This letter is easy to write and I feel lighter and lighter as I write. I print it out, roll it up and tie a green (green being the colour of forgiveness, so says Google) string around it, the same type of green string that Robin tied around my wrist as my slightly flawed tether before I left for overseas. I then head off down the street, where I buy a large bunch of white roses, a large mixed bunch of roses and three small scented candles.

I pack everything up in a little bag and put it in the hall, ready.

Holding dear

Susannah

There is a framed photo of Mum that sits on the side table in our living room. It is one of the last photos of her before she became really sick, and it is beautiful. Taken on her last Christmas she is sitting on a bench in the park outside Mum and Dad's house watching all her children and grandchildren play a game of cricket. She is laughing, her eyes shining, and she is happy as she keeps watch over her clan. Edvard took the photo and we each – Dad, Duncan, Sophie and me – have one in our living room. It keeps her close; it keeps her on watch over us.

Before I go to bed I take the bunch of beautiful white roses and split them over three vases. I take one vase and put it on the bedside table in the guest room for Robin and I put another on the table where we will have our Mother's Day dinner. The last vase of roses I put next to the photo of Mum. I sit on the sofa and, in my head, I thank her for everything she gave me and for the love that healed me and that now makes it possible for me to forgive Robin and accept her also as my mother. An angry wounded heart finds it hard, maybe impossible, to forgive: a heart softened with love is

305

more able to stay open and let people in. Mum and Dad made my heart soft again.

I tell Mum my plans for the next day and I feel her love and her blessing. Sitting there, I feel close to Mum, and this makes me both happy and sad. I cry a bit and the pain of missing her that is never far away stabs my heart. I kiss my finger and lay it on her photo.

I go to bed and sleep well. Peacefully.

Mother's Day 2015

Susannah

Nine months (another crazy coincidence) after we meet and it seems, finally, Robin and I have found both some solid ground and a lighter place to be. Now a mock-orange plant – like the one outside Robin's bedroom – grows by the day bed on the Longleaf verandah; and in Robin's front garden, looking over the orchid I gave her for her birthday, grows a pot of mint for my herbal tea. I no longer need my navigation device to get to Robin's house, nor she her Melways to get to mine – and she is coming over for Mother's Day dinner and to stay the night.

On Mother's Day morning I wake early and go to the living room. I light one of the small candles in front of Mum's picture and next to her white roses, give her a kiss and wish her a happy Mother's Day. I then go back to bed where I await my own Mother's Day greetings from Emma. She makes me one of her beautiful heart cards.

Edvard arrives with flowers and a big hug and we all head off for a Mother's Day lunch at one of my favourite restaurants. I love Mother's Day – even often contrary teenage children know that, just for that day, they have to be nice to Mum, laugh at her jokes, take her advice and give her hugs and kisses. I float the idea that a maternal virtue might be extolled every thirty minutes during the lunch but this, apparently, is pushing my luck. Oh well, worth a try, and the lunch is brilliant anyway with my children, my family, happy and relaxed in each other's company.

Robin

My Mother's Day is quiet and peaceful. I live alone and my daughters have their own families, so I cannot get my prized morning cup of tea brought to me in bed. Instead, I get it myself and quickly scurry back to bed so that I can almost believe it was brought to me after all: 'Thank you, darling (any darling), that's lovely.'

All four daughters ring to wish me happy Mother's Day and have chosen gifts that, each in their own way, express both them and me and reflect the uniqueness of our respective relationships. A precious variety; I am blessed.

I am going to Susannah's later in the afternoon and will have dinner there. In her usual caring way she has taken pains to cater to my tastes and has cooked the meal of my choice: lamb chops, mashed potato and tinned peas. When it comes to the crunch, I abandon the more sophisticated tastes acquired later in life and revert unerringly to the culinary loves of my childhood.

Susannah has also planned a ceremony for us to officially mark and seal the fact of our reunion and her forgiveness of me for having given her away. I think it is a wonderful idea. My only reservation is the fact that she has chosen the beach as the site of the ceremony, which I get completely as far as symbolism goes, but where the spirit is willing, the flesh is weak and my flesh is already quailing in light of the weather forecast for thirteen degrees, wind and rain.

Susannah

I have decided the ceremony needs to be at the beach, the beach where I have spent so much time walking, running and thinking through the past year's problems and joys. Robin has read the weather report and is less decided. I point out to her that it is my forgiveness ritual and she graciously concedes, saying she will bring wet-weather gear.

Robin arrives and we head off. The wind is ferocious and a storm threatens. It is remarkably like the weather that lashed Federation Square and us the day Robin and I met. And, once again, Robin is compliant about following me out into the storm.

We drive the short distance to the beach and head out on the jetty, the wind almost lifting us as we walk. But I press on. I stop at the end of the jetty. We are alone – obviously; who else would be here in this weather? – and I set up.

I take the last two scented candles and place them in a metal box. My original vision was for them to be burning free in the open air but, in these now nearly cyclonic conditions, this idea is clearly doomed. I tell Robin that one candle is for me and one is for her and I tell her I want to read her something.

'Robin', I start, voice already a bit shaky as I read, 'I now fully recognise the pain you caused me when you left me and forgot about me. And each of these stones represents that.'

As I say each word I take a stone and throw it into the ocean. It sounds rather poetic but it's actually clunky as I try to balance my bag, my stones and piece of paper in the howling wind. This is not how it played in my head when I planned it. There, it was more beautiful and less shambolic. Yet there is still a satisfying moment as each stone hits the water. I carry on.

'The fear and panic of abandonment, the sadness and confusion of loss, the resentment and regret for what might have been, the feelings of insecurity, of unworthiness, of not being good enough.

'I have held them in my heart for long enough.

'I now release them all. They are no longer part of me.

'I now let go of all hurt and anger that I have held against you in my mind, my body and my heart.

'I am completely enough. I am worthy of being loved and I am free to love wholeheartedly.

'And I'm free to love you for the beautiful, caring, wise and brave woman I see you are now, to accept the love you give me now and embrace the joy of our reunion.

'So, I truly forgive you, Robin.

'Completely.

'The baby who screamed for you is quiet now.

'The toddler who asked about you has been answered.

'The child who wondered about you knows.

'The young woman who denied you sees you.

'And I now come to you in forgiveness and love.

'We all forgive you completely and unconditionally.

'Please forgive me for any pain my anger and hurt has caused you.

'I love you.'

I set the letter and the paper bag alight with the candle and throw them up in to the air and out to sea. Again the poetic gesture is slightly compromised by the elements, as my flying bonfire threatens to fly back in our faces, but then it too heads out to sea.

Robin

Ducking slightly to avoid the airborne cinders, I suppose it would be easy to mock this rather chaotic little ceremony: to see only its amusing weaknesses and miss its strength. The movies would do it so fabulously: the candles lit and glowing in the warm stillness of the perfect evening, the burning fire on the water carried out to sea. Such beauty! Such a feeling of significance!

I appreciate and enjoy aesthetic beauty but have come to realise that externals mean very little and can be deceiving: all that glitters is not gold. Don't judge a book by its cover. It's what's in the human heart that really counts.

So, in a way I relish the apparent 'epic fail' of our forgiveness ceremony, because we aren't here for the success of the ritual, for the aesthetics, or for the perfection of performance – we are here as two imperfect people, sincerely desiring and choosing to forgive and to love each other. Every one of Susannah's lovely words comes from her heart and hits the mark. I receive them and they make me cry.

'Thank you for your forgiveness, Susannah,' I say, holding both her hands. 'I am sorry for all the pain I caused you. I love you.'

Susannah

We hug. I blow out the candles and give one to Robin, and then I suggest we go quickly back to the car. She needs no further encouragement.

Driving back, I look at my poor windswept other mother and wonder if all this was a good idea. It certainly hasn't gone the way I planned. But then again, on this journey with Robin that I didn't even know I was going on, what has? What ever does?

And I suspect that there will be more tattered visions, more moments that don't quite work as Robin and I muddle on, but the forgiveness 'thing' has done its work and we are at once cut loose from the past and anchored for the future.

When we come home, Robin stands in front of the beautiful open fire my lovely and long-suffering Oskar has prepared for us and I give her a bunch of mixed roses.

'Happy Mother's Day, Robin!'

My mother-heart is filled and my daughter-heart is truly blessed. Some people don't even get one mother who loves them completely. I get two.

Finally, all heartlines are open and I am home.

Acknowledgements

No one ever does anything by themselves. We are very grateful to all the lovely people who helped us do this book.

Obviously, it would have been impossible without our family. We thank them for allowing us to include little bits of their story in our story and for their kindness and care in reading various drafts. So, thank you all, with love: Ada, Anna, Aziza, Ben, Billie, Brian, Charmayne, Claudia, Declan, Dominique, Dougall, Duncan, Dylan, Edvard, Emma, Felix, Finn, Florence, Henrietta, Hjalmar, Jake, Jason, Joel, Levi, Maja, Marian, Matilda, Matthieu, Naomi, Oliver, Oskar, Pam, Sam, Sophie, Stina, Sten, Susan, Theo, Tim R and Tim S.

With special thanks, but no royalties, to Brian and Tim, for their cameos.

Bethany, for all her support and mind-mapping.

Ali, Andrea, Anita, Maddy, Rebecca and Tom, for reading various drafts and for their honest feedback.

Rebecca, for her beautiful photos.

Krissy Fry, for her calm wisdom and care, with much gratitude.

Meredith, for wanting to publish the book, and Brandon and Claire for their editorial cleverness in helping make it a better one.

We also thank the copyright holders for their permission to reproduce material.

All emails and correspondence from the Department of Health and Human Services are © State of Victoria, Australia and reproduced with permission of the Secretary to the Department of Health and Human Services. Reproduction and other uses comprised in the copyright are prohibited without permission.

Thanks to Gwinganna Lifestyle Retreat for permission to recount the content of their seminar.

Extracts from *Four Quartets* and *The Waste Land* by T.S. Eliot reproduced with the permission of Faber and Faber Ltd.